TE DUE

FROM WEST TO EAST

University of Illinois Press, Urbana and London, 1966

FROM

ROBERT EDSON LEE

WEST TO EAST

Studies
in the Literature of
the American West

for Marc DuPlan Lee and John Edwards Lee

ACKNOWLEDGMENTS

For permission to use certain copyrighted materials, I thank the following: The Academy of American Franciscan History, publisher of Tibesar's work on Serra; American Book Company, publisher of Williams and Simpson, eds., *Washington Irving on the Prairie*; The Belknap Press of Harvard University Press, publisher of the Holman edition of Simms's *Views and Reviews*; Malcolm Cowley; The Ralph Waldo Emerson Memorial Association; Harper & Row, Publishers, Inc., publisher of Wade's *Francis Parkman*, DeVoto's edition of *Mark Twain in Eruption*, Albert Bigelow Paine's biography of Mark Twain, and Paine's edition of *Mark Twain's Letters*; Houghton Mifflin Company, publisher of Norton and Howe's *Letters of Charles Eliot Norton*, Cather's *O Pioneers!*, and DeVoto's *Across the Wide Missouri* and *The Course of Empire*; Mark Twain Company and Huntington Library Publications, publisher of Dixon Wecter, ed., *Mark Twain to Mrs. Fairbanks*, copyright 1949 by the Mark Twain Company; A. A. Knopf, publisher of the 1932 edition of Flint's *Recollections*, Walker and Dane, eds., *Mark Twain's Travels with Mr. Brown*, and publisher of the Cather quotations in Kates, ed., *Willa Cather in Europe* and Cather's *Not Under Forty* and *On Writing*; Macmillan Company, publisher of Howard Doughty, *Francis Parkman*, copyright 1962; Mrs. Garrett Mattingly; The Quivira Society, publisher of the Hodge translation of Villagrá; The Board of Trustees of Leland Stanford Junior University which first published the Wallace Stegner essay, "Benny DeVoto's America" in Julian Barclay, ed., *The Papers of Bernard DeVoto*, reprinted in *Four Portraits and One Subject: Bernard DeVoto*; University of California Press, publisher of Smith and Anderson, eds., *Mark Twain of the Enterprise*; University of Nebraska Press, publisher of Bennett's *The World of Willa Cather* (Bison Book edition, copyright 1961), Cather's *Collected Short Fiction*, copyright 1965, and Cather's "When I Knew Stephen Crane." Special thanks are due Mrs. Bernard DeVoto for kind permission to publish numerous quotations from the work of Bernard DeVoto.

Contents

"His spirit was essentially Western; and herein is his peculiar Americanism; for the Western spirit is, or will yet be (for no other is, or can be), the true American one."

— Melville

"Hitherto, the movement of enlightenment has been from east to west. The inhabitants of the United States, if they do not reject this destiny, will one day halt and reverse this movement."

— Bernard Lacépède

"'T is pedantry to estimate nations by the census, or by square miles of land, or other than by their importance to the mind of the time."

— Emerson

1

FROM EAST TO WEST

The concern of this book can best be expressed metaphorically in the image of Western man straddling his vast empire in splendor, yet standing with his back to the West and looking eastward with awe and reverence toward his superannuated past. This giant is inarticulate and so tamed that he hardly knows his own thralldom. He has wonders to tell, but he stands mute. But even that image is a fantastic exaggeration, a typical product of the giant-imagining West, not true to fact. A hundred years elapsed in the American West before a native literate person was produced. The interim involved Easterners who came as explorers or tourists to the West, who showed some awareness of that unique and lovely country, but who, in the process of returning to the more "cultured" East and translating the firsthand experience into an acceptable terminology, altered that unique experience into some lesser thing. The romantic urge of the East, the illusion-making power of words, changed the image of the West from one thing into another. From the point of view of the West — and only the stance is different in this study, the notion of looking from West to East — the literature of the American West has a different aspect. Consider the West as a foreign country, utterly strange and blank, and observe the process of expression, the translation of a perishable experience into inadequate words.

At the outset we have to delimit the West. It was, originally, anything west of the Alleghenies, some breath-taking mysterious quality inherent in the unknown. In time, the West became more geographically and realistically restricted, though it was still spiritually vague. Where does the West begin — the western suburbs of Chicago? the Mississippi? the Missouri? the 100th meridian? the irregular line of the Great Plains? the Rocky Mountains? Which of these represents the border between one country and the other? Mark Twain, riding the stage between St. Joseph, Missouri, and Fort Kearny, found that he had crossed a border in 1862 when the breakfast talk went like this: " 'Pass the bread, you son of a skunk!' No, I forget — skunk was not the word; it seems to me it was still stronger than that; I know it was, in fact, but it is gone from my memory, apparently. However, it is no matter — probably it was too strong for print, anyway. It is the landmark in my memory which tells me where I first encountered the vigorous new vernacular of the occidental plains and mountains."[1] Decades later, Willa Cather's border was only a little more distinct: "Whenever I crossed the Missouri River coming into Nebraska the very smell of the soil tore me to pieces."[2] In fact, a new cultural region begins where geographic conditions change the basic factors in land settlement. In the 1840's and 1850's, eastern population pressures drove settlement beyond the verge of forest onto the treeless plains, such that today there is still a distinct difference between Dakota and Minnesota (Sinclair Lewis' Wheatsylvania, North Dakota, in *Arrowsmith* is vastly dif-

[1] Mark Twain, *Roughing It*, in *The Writings of Mark Twain*, Author's National Edition (25 vols.; New York: Harper, 1907-18), VII, 27-28. In general, only the first appearance of a primary source is given footnote citation. All secondary sources are credited by footnotes.

[2] Willa Cather, quoted by Mildred R. Bennett, *The World of Willa Cather* (New York: Dodd, Mead, 1951), p. 138.

ferent from his Gopher Prairie, Minnesota, in *Main Street*), Nebraska and Iowa, Kansas and Missouri, Oklahoma and Arkansas, Texas and Louisiana. So, arbitrarily, I use that line between two tiers of states as the beginning of the West.

This high-handed definition still leaves a big country: seventeen states and 1.8 million square miles of land, far more than the land mass of all of Europe. The distinctive area may be clearer if we place Europe over a map of the West and observe similarities. To the north are Scandinavian forests and fisheries. East are the steppes of Russia. French vineyards are in the west; the mineral Ruhr is central, near the mountains of Switzerland. South are the Spanish plains or the citrus of North Africa; southeast is the oil of Turkey. The sizes are comparable. Yet the population of Europe today is some 400 million and the population of the seventeen states is a mere 44 million, and this betrays a distinguishing characteristic of the West — its relatively uninhabited space. The whole West is broken apart and separated by the vast upheaval of the Rocky Mountains and blocked again by the Cascades and the Sierra Nevada farther west. It is cracked into bottomless canyons — the Snake, the Grand, the Columbia — and its center is one huge saline desert across Utah and Nevada, in Idaho and Arizona. The density of population of Nevada in 1960 was still only 2.6 persons per square mile — and that was 70 per cent urban. Discount Las Vegas (where one drives down the garish Strip at night in blinding waves of blowing sand); discount the stench of diesel oil and the broken beer bottles on the highways; the central fact of the West is still the uninterrupted flat horizon in every direction, an empty space such that at night an observer may see only one light or none. The typical landscape of the West is not the megopolis in California, but the red rock of desert, as old as Egypt yet almost unmarked by man's antiquity. The seventeen countries of the West are isolated and separate, tied not by the highways and railroads but by the sweeping wind. Wind and space, space measured by some lone barren rock, these are the West. And the sun: for the other distinguishing characteristic of the West is its aridity. Despite the rain forests of Oregon, despite the ski slopes of Colorado, and despite Nebraska, which ironically has the greatest river mileage of any state in the Union, the dominant tone of the West is set by its lack of rain. The first reports of the region as a desert as large and dry as the Sahara were not far from wrong. Arable land in the West is but a small per cent of its land mass. The population of the West strains for water, its mechanical ingenuity brought up abruptly by fixed, eternal, harsh maximums beyond which is left only the salt of the ocean. Rock, wind, space, and sun circumscribe man in the West; in some unknown way they affect his character and, in turn, his writing.

But the West is not as proportionately vast in time as it is in space. *American* history of the West (as here delimited) can be said to begin exactly in October, 1800, when one Philip Nolan and twenty companions crossed into the future Texas to hunt wild mustangs. It is the starting date I will use here for the distinctively *American* experience. However, the written history of the West predates the American entry; it predates Drake or Shakespeare in the considerable body of essentially *Spanish* literature. These were men reacting to experiences in the same country, and perhaps we can discover in them predictions of the way Americans will write, the trends or the ingrained limitations of the future literature. More likely it will turn out to be the limitations of the Spanish point of view, useful because it is in contrast to the American. It concerns gold and souls.

The Spanish settlements in California, Arizona, New Mexico, and Texas were the late weak northern extension of the Spanish invasion of Latin America begun in 1518. Our American concern begins with the avariciousness of one Pánfilo de Narváez, whose voyage after rumors of gold left stranded on Galveston Island in 1528 one Álvar Núñez Cabeza de Vaca, who then wandered across Texas, New Mexico, and Arizona before he arrived at Culiacán in 1536 to make his report. The

Naufragios ("Shipwrecks") of Cabeza de Vaca, more literary than real, contained fantastic hints of gold. His report was "verified" in1539 by the *Relación* of the Franciscan friar Marcos de Niza — known to later historians as the "Lying Monk" — and this was enough to instigate the expedition of Francisco Vásquez de Coronado, who started off eagerly in 1540 in search of the Seven Cities of Cibola, so naively magnified by Cabeza de Vaca and Fray Marcos. Their journals were not so much false as they were capable of being misread. The vast, arid, rocky country could be ignored if one had heard rumors of gold. Fray Marcos, fearing for his life, did not actually go into Cibola, but he saw it from a distant hill and reported that it looked larger than Mexico City. Coronado needed no further report.

The first phase of Spanish-American literature is thus almost a fictionalized series of journals of exploration, gilded by writer and reader alike. That literary readiness for phantasy extended into the seventeenth century. By 1538 there was a University at Santo Tomás; by 1539, a printing press in Mexico; and the Baroque moved from Spain to Mexico along with the means of writing. Thus it should not surprise us to find a "history" of New Mexico written in verse, modeled on the classic *La Araucana* of Zúñiga.

The *Historia de la Nueva Mexico* of Gaspar Pérez de Villagrá, 1610, is a survey of military Spain in New Mexico, culminating in the attack on Acoma Pueblo in 1599. These feats are told in some thirty-four cantos of labored endecasyllabic verse which translate for us most readably in prose. The European shape given to an American experience is clearly evident in the Homeric descriptions of battle, the superhuman struggles with exhortatory interludes — the fantastic formal posturings of a litterateur. Villagrá, though a graduate of the University of Salamanca, was more a soldier than a poet; he found the pen "a new and strange implement to wield" [3]

[3] F. W. Hodge, ed., *History of New Mexico, by Gasper Pérez de Villagrá, Alcalá, 1610* (Los Angeles: The Quivira Society, 1933), 267. Further quotations from this text are not footnoted.

and prayed "that the spirits of those mighty heroes of whom I sing will animate and give me courage and speed my pen along its daring flight, that my words may be worthy of their deeds." Alas, Villagrá could do no more than report that a heaven-sent messenger with a long white beard, a bald head, and a flaming sword, accompanied by a maiden of most wondrous beauty, had been sent by the Holy Mother to aid them in battle. The romantic tendency obscures the facts.

This is true in prose journals too. Witness the arrival of the colonizing army of Governor Don Juan de Oñate at the Rio Grande border in 1598. Mass was celebrated, followed by a drama on the advent of the friars to New Mexico, written by one Captain Farfán and acted by the soldiers. It is no wonder that with such a lovely romantic approach Spain could produce no great lasting colony in the Southwest. These people were blind to the facts of existence. But a literary tradition or pose is established, a folderol approach which colors Southwestern writing even today.

The colonizing of Oñate and others brought some 3,000 Spanish settlers to the future New Mexico by 1680; these were thrown out in the Indian Rebellion of that year, but they surged in again in larger numbers following the reconquest by Governor Diego de Vargas in 1694. By 1740 an estimated 10,000 people of Spanish descent lived in Texas and New Mexico — but in a virtual state of inanimation until the Mexican Revolution of 1821. In the late eighteenth century the colonizing energy was transferred to California, where some ten missions and three towns were established by 1800. There a third type of Spanish writing can be found in the diaries and letters of the honest, hard-working Franciscan fathers.

The most noted is Fray Junípero Serra, who said himself that "half my life is spent writing letters."[4] Fray Serra, a Franciscan professor at Mallorca, heard there a recruiter for

[4] Quoted by Antonine Tibesar, O.F.M., ed., *Writings of Junípero Serra* (6 vols.; Washington, D.C.: Academy of American Franciscan History, 1955-56), I, xvi. Further quotations from this text are not footnoted.

missionaries, and in 1749, thirsting for martyrdom, he headed for Mexico. He spent years in the pagan region of Sierra Gorda (where he reported witches to the Inquisition of Mexico City) and years more at the College of San Fernando training missionary novices. Finally, in 1767, with the banishment of the Jesuits from missions in Baja California, Serra moved toward the frontier and in 1769 headed into New California. Before his death in 1784 he had founded nine missions and baptized 4,307 persons. His life is described in his letters and diary, in the biography of his contemporary Fray Francisco Palou, and in the *Relación Histórica* (1787). Serra's success lay in his faith, in his great physical energy (he was small and crippled), and in his ability to beg supplies from the church authorities in Mexico City. His letters are lively and personal, describing in concrete details his hardships: "Seeing that Your Excellency has already ordered a forge to be brought in the last shipload for San Diego Mission — which, after many difficulties, I succeeded in having delivered by the Officer — one thing yet remains: that Your Excellency should send a blacksmith there." These are the words of a man relying more on hard work than on miracle. His entire motive — the harvest of souls — indicates how different he was from the American movement which was to follow: "You could not wish for anything more touching than the love that these gentiles have for the good Fathers. . . . Very many ask, and they are earnest about it, to be baptized. And so I say with regard to these people, as I do of the others, that when we are in a position to provide them with a moderate amount of food, and if the bad example and annoyances caused by the soldiers do not corrupt them, we may hope within a short time to see a multitude of Christians." Perhaps between the thirst for gold and the thirst for souls, Spanish-American writing prior to 1800 can be summed up as Baroque (not native), fictional (not by intent), epistolary, and of little permanent influence on the America to come. Spain had left indelible cultural marks in the Southwest, but no memorable literature.

This is sad, for as Villagrá pointed out: "No greater misfortune could possibly befall a people than to lack a historian
properly to set down their annals; one who with faithful zeal
will guard, treasure, and perpetuate all those human events
which if left to the frail memory of man and to the mercy of
the passing years will be sacrificed upon the altars of time."
If this was partly the fate of the several thousand of Spanish
descent in America, it was the fatal tragedy for the million
aborigines. A people who cannot write cannot survive. Artifacts, pictographs, and oral legends are but the ghosts, the
symbols of man. One could almost say that it was permissible
to destroy the American Indian because he had no literature
— no past, other than animal. Salish, Siouan, Caddoan, Sha-
haptin, Shapwailutan, Hokan, Shoshonean, Algonquian, Pe-
nutian, Kiowan, Tanoan, Yuman, Piman — these are but the
major linguistic divisions in the Indian West, and there are
scores of tribal subdivisions, hardly given names before the
anthropologists of our time. And though the Western Indian
has been to school for a century, he has still not written a
memorable word. This is a shockingly broad generalization,
and there is no literary study of Indian writing to back it up.
In this work, however, we can only remark the absence of a
literature by the natives in the West and thus admit the pre-
posterous flamboyant colorings of Cooper's fiction as a starting point, with the countless interpretations of The Indian
which followed, written by genteel asses. The Red Man,
Adam in the Garden, has vanished without a word.

If this were a survey of the literature of the West, we would
turn next to the French, to the *Jesuit Relations* insofar as the
Jesuits crossed the border of the future America; or turn to
the record of explorers like Pierre Gaultier de Varennes,
Sieur de La Vérendrye, and his son Louis-Joseph. We would
have to examine then the journals and trade records of the
British who encroached on American land via the Pacific
Ocean or by Canada, James Cook, George Vancouver, or Alexander Mackenzie; but if we did we might never reach 1800.

There is no literary study as such of the Spanish, the French, and the English, literary and restricted to the American borders, and probably there is no reason for one. All three belong to other traditions than ours, and Lewis and Clark did not learn literary style from Villagrá. (Nor is there, by the way, any extended literary history of the West *after* 1800, though there ought to be.) What I intend here is to indicate the range of response available, to indicate that the usual pattern would seem to be to import a literary technique or point of view as, of course, the best means of communicating with the parent culture. Some penchant for fantasy may be traceable to the influence of the West itself, but more likely that golden vision of the Spaniards was imported too. The base for writing is necessarily the letter home, the report or journal; and the exploits, by a personal necessity of ego-building, will be enlarged and embroidered into a formal history. These writers, at any rate, were not concerned to see things as they are, and we can safely predict that the romantic nineteenth century will have passed before anyone is much concerned in the West about reality.

Perhaps we need Tocqueville to remind us that the problem of the relation of West to East is but an extension of the problem of the relation of the New World to the Old. Writing in 1840, he found in the United States no literature, because the American was still imitating his English ancestors: "The larger part of that small number of men in the United States who are engaged in the composition of literary works are English in substance, and still more so in form. Thus they transport into the midst of democracy the ideas and literary fashions which are current among the aristocratic nation they have taken for their model. They paint with colours borrowed from foreign manners; and as they hardly ever represent the country they were born in as it really is, they are seldom popular there."[5]

[5] Alexis de Tocqueville, *Democracy in America*, Henry Steele Commager, ed. (London: Oxford, 1946), p. 328.

My concern here is with the men and women, Western or Eastern, who traveled into a new country, who responded in some way to the particular quality of the West, but who were unable, for a variety of reasons, to transform the first-hand experience of history into a literature of their own.

2

THE JOURNALISTS:
Lewis and Clark

Their luggage was supply enough for more than two years — a miscellany of ammunition, gewgaws for the Indians, carpenter tools, and medicines. In retrospect, certain objects are significant: the fiddle, the tin trumpets, the sword, the folding boat, the portable soup, the air gun, the mercury for the cure of venereal disease, and a desk. These were the symbols of American exploration which had to be pulled up the Missouri River to its source, lugged across the Rocky Mountains on horseback, floated down the Snake and Columbia rivers, and then returned — with the addition of the journals, the transcript of one of man's greatest adventures, the very stuff of literature.

Back east, certain artifacts, including a live "burrowing squirrel" or black-tailed prairie dog, ended up on display at Monticello or in Peale's Museum in Philadelphia. Certain skins had been lost to fleas. Some seeds were given to the wealthy gardener, William Hamilton. But the journals, after much delay, were given to a dilettante litterateur from Philadelphia, who, in keeping with the true spirit of his times, dutifully condensed, bowdlerized, prettified, and emasculated into a shoddy lifeless prose the grandest of all records of American endeavor. From the point of view of the West, the East caged and tamed the history of the Lewis and Clark expedition, rather like the "burrowing squirrel" so confined by Peale.

Initially, the expedition involved a literary problem. A military company of some thirty-five men was to be sent into the West beyond where white man had been before but where America must inevitably go. They were to seek out and then spell out one of the vast unknown areas of the world. Their record, their impress would literally determine the future of a people. How should one speak of such endeavor?

It was Jefferson who ordered it, who prescribed the style and form and content of the future journals. Aware of the physical dangers involved, he specified to Lewis, "Your observations [of latitude and longitude] are to be taken with great pains & accuracy, to be entered distinctly, & intelligibly . . . several copies of these, as well as your other notes, should be made at leisure times & put into the care of the most trustworthy of your attendants, to guard by multiplying them, against the accidental losses to which they will be exposed."[1] His directive reflects the rational approach of a deist who based his beliefs on the accurate observation of fact. It anticipates the marvelous logic of the journals; for example, "The inferrence therefore deduced from those premices are that the best and most Practicable rout across the Continent. . . ." Jefferson, the amateur scientist, questioned his scientist friends. What would they like to know about the new country? To the physician Dr. Benjamin Rush he wrote, "It would be very useful to state for him [Lewis] those objects on which it is most desirable he should bring us information." To another physician, Dr. Caspar Wistar, he wrote,

[1] Reuben Gold Thwaites, ed., *Original Journals of the Lewis and Clark Expedition, 1804–1806* (8 vols.; New York: Dodd, Mead, 1904–5), VII, 248. Future quotations from this source are not footnoted.

"I have thought it would be useful to confine his [Lewis'] attention to those objects only on which information is most deficient & most desirable: & therefore would thank you to make a note on paper of those which occur to you as most desirable for him to attend to." And to Lewis, the formal instructions spelled out in detail the scientific areas of inquiry: the rivers, the surrounding country, the aborigines and artifacts, the climate, the animals, the minerals; these can be translated as geography, anthropology and ethnology, climatology, zoology, botany, geology — see, in short, Jefferson's own *Notes on Virginia* (1784), for the breadth of his eighteenth-century curiosity.

Moreover, Jefferson had trained his man for two years, anticipating the expedition. Captain Meriwether Lewis, known to Jefferson through Virginia family connections, had served as Jefferson's private secretary. Indoctrinated into the international world of science and the American political scene, to say nothing of the niceties of neoclassic prose, the secretary echoed the President. Their letters, except for spelling, are interchangeable. Lewis to Jefferson: "accept the assureance of my sincere wishes for your health and happiness." Jefferson to Lewis: "accept my affectionate salutations & assurances of constant esteem." Jefferson trained his man in observation, in writing, in scientific method, in diplomacy, in all but spelling and mental stability. Lewis, by Jefferson's account, was "subject to hypochondriac affections" and "sensible depressions of mind."[2] Jefferson must have weighed this as well as the dangers of the proposed expedition and ordered up a duplicate captain, presumably to guard the personnel as well as the papers by multiplying them against accidental loss.

Thus began the absolutely unique military unit with two captains. The authority of the two was equal. As Lewis wrote

[2] Thomas Jefferson, "Life of Captain Lewis," in Paul Allen, ed., *History of the Expedition Under the Command of Captains Lewis and Clark* (Philadelphia: Bradford and Inskeep, 1814), pp. xliii–xliv. This is the so-called Biddle edition of the journals. Future quotations from this source are not footnoted.

Clark, "your situation if joined with me in this mission will in all respects be precisely such as my own." Yet Lewis out-ranked Clark; when Clark's commission came through, it specified only a second lieutenancy; the "captain" was honorary.[3] Lewis was the confidant of the President, the first chosen, the better educated. Yet for two years, the two men were as close as Damon and Pythias, an exact counterbalance of minds, working together without any friction whatever. A part of our interest in the journals is the sparkling interplay of these men, the introvert Lewis and the extrovert Clark, a large figure in combination, the first bifurcated giant of the West. They wrote the journals together, in every possible combination: Lewis' record, Clark's record, Lewis' version of Clark's record, Clark's version of Lewis'. The character of each captain comes out clearly; it is the essence of the literary quality of the journals.

But before closer investigation of Lewis and Clark, it is proper to recall the other men who kept journals, in order to better admire the perspicacity of Jefferson's choice. Lewis wrote to Jefferson from Fort Mandan: "I have sent a journal kept by one of the Sergeants, to Capt Stoddard, my agent at St Louis, in order as much as possible to multiply the chances of saving something. we have encouraged our men to keep journals, and seven of them do so, to whom in this respect we give every assistance in our power." The expedition antici-pates the numerous writing generals of World War II. All seven journals have not survived, but there are journals of four: Sergeants Floyd, Gass, Ordway, and Private White-house. These are uniformly perfunctory and poor, useful only as historical supplements to the journals of the captains, but very revealing by contrast.

The briefest is the journal of poor Sergeant Charles Floyd, who died on August 20, 1804, some 12,000 words out of St. Louis. His journal is distinguished only by its vastly inferior

[3] Donald Jackson, ed., *Letters of the Lewis and Clark Expedition, with Related Documents, 1783–1854* (Urbana: University of Illinois Press, 1962), 172n.

spelling: "fog" is "fague"; "which" is "hough"; "usual hour"
is "yousel ouer"; "gentle breeze" is "Jentel Breas." The loss of
Floyd, the only white man to die on the expedition, is no loss
to literature.

Sergeant Patrick Gass's journal covers the entire journey in
some 80,000 words. It is too perfunctory and too matter-of-
fact to be of literary interest. Moreover, the only extant version is the rewrite by David McKeehan, a schoolmaster, which
is described by one scholar as "horribly 'literary,'"[4] but is
more typically simply flat. For example, here is the entire entry for February 9, 1806: "We had a fine morning; but in the
course of the day we had sometimes sunshine, and sometimes
showers of rain. One of our hunters caught a beaver."[5] It simply is not very informative. Gass was named sergeant on
Floyd's death, but his journal does not improve on Floyd's.

Sergeant John Ordway recorded the entire journey in some
100,000 words. His version of the expedition seems to be ade-
quate as a record, but it is in many ways simply a less vivid
rewrite of the journal of Clark. Time and again Ordway re-
counted the events of a day in the same order and in words
similar to those of Clark.[6] He used less detail and, of course,
he was in a subordinate position, so that his journal is passive,
not commanding. Ordway's is a record only, with no value as
literature.

Private Joseph Whitehouse in 67,000 words covers the expedition only until its arrival at the ocean in November, 1805.
Actually, his journal is a collective affair, written by three dif-

[4] John E. Bakeless, *Lewis & Clark, Partners in Discovery* (New
York: W. Morrow, 1947), p. 120.

[5] Patrick Gass, *A Journal of the Voyages and Travels of a Corps of
Discovery, 1807*, Earle R. Forrest, ed. (Minneapolis: Ross & Haines,
1958), p. 222.

[6] Milo M. Quaife, ed., *The Journals of Captain Meriwether Lewis
and Sergeant John Ordway*, Wisconsin Historical Society, *Collections*,
XXII (Madison: State Historical Society, 1916). For an example of
word-for-word rewrite, see Clark's entry for June 29, 1805, Thwaites,
II, 198–200, and Ordway in Quaife, pp. 239–240.

ferent hands.[7] Whoever writer No. 2 was, he could not spell.
"Prairie" is given as "Prarie," "Perarie," and "perara." Writer
No. 3 spelled "Missouri" as "Mesury" and "Mussiry" in the
same paragraph that *he* spelled "prairie" as "preare." Spelling
eccentricities are amusing but no valid reason for our concern,
however. The lack of value of the minor journals can be indicated by parallel quotations. Whitehouse's entry for October 1, 1804, is:

Set off eairly. a cloudy morning fare wind. we Sailed on
rapidly. at 9 oClock we passed dog River which comes in on
S.S. we Camped on a Sand bar in the middle of the river, a
french trador comes to us from the S. Shore.

Clark's entry for the day, after some three hundred words of
description, reaches the "trador" in this way:

we Saw a man opposit to our Camp on the L.S. which we discov[d]
to be a Frenchman, a little of[f] (*from Shore among*) the Willows
we observed a house, we Call to them to come over, a boy came
in a canoe & informed that 2 frenchmen were at the house with
good[s] to trade with the Seauex.

Later in the evening the trader visited the camp and Clark
summarizes the gossipy information on the country ahead.
"The black mountains he Says is verry high, and Some parts
of it has Snow on it in the Summer." It is a lengthy scene, one
we can visualize, charged with the emotion of the strangeness
ahead, a precise record of a moment in history. Clark dwelt on
detail. He could write narrative. He had a lively curiosity.
And Lewis was usually better than Clark. No sergeant or
private could equal the vision of the captains. The other men
lacked power of observation. They generalized where Lewis
and Clark specified. They were subordinates in rank and in
mental perceptiveness; their individuality was subdued by
their lack of education as well as by their peripheral status.
And they point up sharply the problem of finding literature
in the West. The writer must be sensitive to what he sees
and sufficiently educated to communicate it. Such uncommon

[7] Identified as such by Thwaites, VII, 34n ff.

experiences were no place for the common man, if we are to have a literature of the past.

Turn now to the journals of Lewis and Clark and the central problem, that is, which of several versions we should read, for they are in multiple form and varying worth. There are three versions: certain field notes or first drafts; the journals or notebook journals; and the Nicholas Biddle rewrite of the journals. The method of writing is of interest here, although our information on the subject is scanty.

The presumption is that both writers kept daily field notes (though there are only fragments by Lewis) written up in the boats or in overnight camps. These field notes were written up in journal form whenever a longer camp was made. Sergeant Floyd noted such a stop on July 25, 1804: "Continued Hear as the Capts is not Don there Riting." This, too, may be the significance of the portable desk which Clark reported broken in an accident on September 15, 1805. These notebook journals were written primarily in books bound in red morocco, each one sealed into a tin box on completion. The scholars Coues and Thwaites, however, decided that the notebook journals were written on the return to St. Louis in 1806, citing among other items Clark's notation of September 26: "a fine morning we commenced writing &c." [8] But Osgood's more recent work is based on the newly discovered field notes of Clark; one can presume that the notebook journals had to be written en route.[9]

The difference between the field notes and the journals can be shown with excerpts from Clark, November 5, 1805. The first draft reads in part:

we are all wet cold and disagreeable, rain continues & encreases. I killed a Pheasent which is very fat. my feet and legs cold. I saw 17 Snakes to day on a Island but little appearance of Frost in this place.

[8] The description of the original journals is by Elliott Coues, in Thwaites, VII, 411–423.

[9] Ernest S. Osgood, ed., *The Field Notes of Captain William Clark, 1803–1805* (New Haven: Yale University Press, 1964), p. xvii.

This was later expanded and reordered to read:

The day proved cloudy with rain the greater part of it, we are all wet cold and disagreeable — I saw but little appearance of frost in this valley. . . . In my walk of to Day I saw 17 Striped Snakes I killed a grouse which was verry fat, and larger than common.

These quotations come from a period in which we have no entries by Lewis. On the only occasion in which three versions exist together — Lewis' journal, Clark's field notes, and Clark's journal, April 16–21, 1806 — the journals are written almost independently, with only one sentence common to both men. Lewis: "twelve horses will be sufficient to transport our baggage and some pounded fish which we intend taking with us as a reserved store for the rocky mountains." Clark's version is slightly different: "twelve horses will be sufficient to transport our baggage and some pounded fish with our dried Elk, which we intend takeing with us as a reserved store for the plains & rocky mountains." This entry does not appear in Clark's first draft, but it does not necessarily follow that it originated in the nonexistent first draft of Lewis, for the journals contain many entries not alluded to in the field notes. Therefore, the sentence could belong to either Lewis or Clark. If it originated with Clark, why did the meticulous Lewis leave out "with our dried Elk" and "plains &"? If with Lewis, why did Clark not copy out "taking" in its correct spelling? It is generally believed that where the journal entries run parallel, it is usually Clark copying the work of Lewis.[10] The simpler vocabulary of Clark (most noticeable in the field notes) would indicate this. But if B is copying A's work with decent spelling, why does he introduce misspellings? The reverse is more likely; if A copies B's work with poor spelling in it, A will correct the misspellings. There is at least the possibility that Lewis copied freely from Clark. The problem can only be solved by judgments on the comparative tones

[10] The matter is discussed in Thwaites, I, xxxv, in Bakeless, p. 299, and in Bernard DeVoto, ed., *The Journals of Lewis and Clark* (Boston: Houghton Mifflin, 1953), p. 312.

of the two writers — which is completely missing in Biddle's synthesis of the two men. It is the immediacy of the field notes and the journals which is my concern here.

Part of the modern reader's interest is in not knowing from day to day what will happen next; a sympathetic tension is brought into play, which makes the journals so particularly fascinating. Thus, when Lewis writes, "after wrighting this imperfect discription I again viewed the falls and was so much disgusted with the imperfect idea which it conveyed of the scene that I determined to draw my pen across it and begin agin, but then reflected that I could not perhaps succeed better than pening the first impressions of the mind," we are there. Or we listen to Clark saying, "in my last rout I lost a part of my notes which could not be found as the wind must have blown them to a great distance," and we have a vivid sense of particular moments. Or, Lewis again, writing from the mountains in August, "the ink f[r]eizes in my pen," elicits our sympathy and participation. It is why we can speak of the journals as literature.

In sum, then, the field notes of Lewis and Clark are as cursory and uninteresting as the work of Floyd, Gass, Ordway, and Whitehouse. The more reflective and detailed journals, expanded from the field notes but written *during* the expedition, are the *literary* source. They, however, must be read in the original and complete version to give a true sense of the expedition, and they should be read in a new way. There are distinct divisions of time and feeling in the expedition, largely ignored by the historians who so carefully repeated the arbitrary equal-length chapter divisions of Nicholas Biddle, although the Edward Biddle and the Voorhis additions make the Nicholas Biddle arrangement of thirty-six chapters even more artificial. A more meaningful grouping can be made as we examine the journals in some detail.

The Edward Biddle collection, discovered in 1913, contains Lewis' journal of his boat trip with a skeleton crew from Pittsburgh to St. Louis, to the arrival at winter quarters, Au-

gust 30–December 12, 1803. It is the appalling record of a
greenhorn. On the very first day out, Lewis stopped at Bru-
not's Island three miles from Pittsburgh to demonstrate his
air gun, which was later to mystify Indians in the West. He
allowed a Mr. Blaze Cenas to discharge the gun; the ball
struck a woman forty yards away. Blood gushed from her
temple, although she soon revived "to our enexpessable satisfaction." [11] On the first day, and the third day, and the fourth,
and the fifth, Lewis' boat became stuck on the ripples or "rif-
fles" in the Ohio, and he had to submit to the pirates who
charged exorbitant prices to haul boats over by means of
horses or oxen. He had to discharge one of his crew, reason
unspecified. His papers and effects were thoroughly wet. He
bought a canoe for $11 and found later that it was too leaky
to use. His men got drunk at night, and the trip was delayed
until they were found, still too drunk at 11:00 A.M. to travel.
Lewis was wet to the skin time and again, and finally was
seized by an ague and fever until he purged himself with
Rush's pills. One can imagine (there is a gap in the journal
of fifty-four days) Lewis being rescued at Louisville by William Clark. It was a shakedown cruise, of course, with the
usual and expected difficulties, but it is interesting to see Lewis as accident-prone or perhaps merely too accustomed to his
sheltered life as Jefferson's secretary.

A second stage of the journey is the time of preparation at
winter quarters. While Lewis stayed south of St. Louis at Ca-
hokia, Clark took the recruits to Camp Dubois on the Illinois shore opposite the mouth of the Missouri River. His recently discovered Dubois journal, December 13, 1803, to
May 14, 1804, has been published by Osgood. Clark, like
Lewis, had his tenderfoot troubles. He was ill and lonely. He
idled away the time with shooting matches or learning to use
the sextant. He fell through the ice and froze his feet. The
chimney of his cabin caught fire. He had trouble with his
men, particularly because of whiskey shops in the neighbor-

[11] Quaife, p. 31.

hood. Clark is seldom voluble, and the Dubois journal is short. But on the whole it was a pleasant winter of anticipation. And when they left, Clark records that many people, "Mail and feeMail," came down to see them off.

The long haul, May 14 to October 24, 1804, to winter quarters at the Mandan villages in central North Dakota, is a third unit, held together by the breathtaking limitless prairies. The wooded east country had begun to open up just beyond St. Louis, and gradually, across the present state of Missouri, the proportions shifted until the grasslands dominated the landscape. Near the mouth of the Des Moines River, Clark noted, "Those Praries are not like those, or a number of those E. of the Mississippi void of every thing except grass." He soon recorded the enchantment of space: "this Plain is verry extensive. . . . The Countrey about this place is butifull." They were all aware of it, even the wooden-prosed sergeants. Gass wrote on June 18: "On the south side there is high land and a long prairie"; on June 22, "We encamped at a handsome prairie . . ."; on July 18, "This is the most open country I ever beheld, almost one continued prairie." Floyd wrote on June 15: "handsom a prarie as ever eney man saw"; on July 4, "we camped at one of the Butifules Praries I ever Saw open and butifulley Divided with Hills and vallies all presenting themselves." Ordway wrote on June 15: "their is Beautiful high Good praries on the South Side/ pleasantest place I have ever Seen"; on July 15, "we could See all around for a long distance in the open praries or as far as our eyes could behold." Farther upriver, Clark recorded, "we beheld a most butifull landscape; Numerous herds of buffalow were Seen feeding in various directions; the Plain to North N.W. & N.E. extends without interuption as far as Can be seen," and still farther north, Lewis wrote in a fragmentary note: "a fine leavel plain extending as far as the eye can reach." These were new dimensions for man, and they were both beautiful and frightening. This is the beginning of a literature which tried to describe the vastly different terms of life in the West, from

Cooper and Irving down to Mari Sandoz, *Love Song to the Plains* (1961).

But with the beauty came the almost insurmountable difficulties of hauling the men in a keelboat and two pirogues up the sixteen hundred miles of the meandering Missouri to the Mandan villages in present-day North Dakota. The journals record the Herculean labor in steamy downpours or blistering heat or contrary winds and blowing sand. As civilization disappeared, the combination of toil and strangeness had its effects. Warner and Hall were absent without leave; Collins was insubordinate; Hall stole whiskey; Collins was drunk on sentry duty; Willard slept on sentry duty; Reed and La Liberté (a civilian in the boat crew) deserted; Newman was insubordinate. Courts-martial were held promptly, and after "inflicting a little punishment" — Clark's laconic phrase for fifty lashes on the "bear" back — they proceeded on. Floyd sickened suddenly and died; Shannon wandered away and was lost and alone on the prairie for some fifteen days, though they sounded the tin trumpets time and again. And they met their first Indians, Sioux, who tested the military strength of the expedition and found it solid. There is no extant Lewis journal for this period. We have only Clark's terse, business-like statements. They contrast sharply with the earlier scatter-brained record of Lewis. This was the period of the expedition that shaped the men — hardened them and unified them by trials. It was a military unit which arrived at the Mandan villages in cold and snow late in October.

There follows a winter interval of six months, again recorded largely but briefly by Clark. It has the tone of a long winter night, the activity of finding enough food and shelter warm enough to keep out the frigid winds, the collecting of information from the Indians, map-making and letter-writing, story-telling — Clark teases us with the statement "Several little Indian aneckd[ts] [anecdotes] told me to day" and nothing more — and a quiet, good-natured busy-ness with the Mandan women, accompanied by drinking and dancing, the fiddle serving its nighttime function. January 10, 1805: "last night was excessively Cold the Murkery this morning Stood at 40° below 0 which is 72° below the freesing point." January 14: "Several men with the Venereal cought from the Mandan women." January 23: "the accurancies [occurrences] of this day is as is common." Never a word from Clark about the increasing tension of the unknown ahead, waiting for the river ice to break up so they could go on. It is a relief to turn from the sketchy Clark to the personal Lewis, now a different man:

The ice in the Missouri has now nearly disappeared. I shall set out on my voyage in the course of a few days. I can foresee no material obstruction to our progress and feel the most perfect confidence that we shall reach the Pacific ocean this summer. For myself, individually, I enjoy better health than I have since I commenced my voyage. The party are now in fine health and excellent spirits, are attached to the enterprise and anxious to proceed. Not a whisper of discontent or murmur is to be heard among them. With such men I feel every confidence necessary to insure success.

And once en route, April 26, he writes:

all in good health, and much pleased at having arrived at this long wished for spot [the mouth of the Yellowstone River], and in order to add in some measure to the general pleasure which seemed to pervade our little community, we ordered a dram to be issued to each person; this soon produced the fiddle, and they spent the evening with much hilarity, singing & dancing, and seemed as perfectly to forget their past toils, as they appeared regardless of those to come.

The mood is one of utmost optimism and joy, enhanced by the uncertainties ahead. How could it have been equaled in the East?

They were now thirty-one men (plus Sacajawea, the wife of the interpreter Charbonneau, and their infant son) in two pirogues and six canoes, with the captains recording what they saw as they moved along. Lewis: "The perogue is so unsteady that I can scarcely write." Lewis: "when we halted for dinner the squaw busied herself in serching for the wild artichokes." Clark: "I saw flowers in the praries to day." By April

14 they had reached "the highest point to which any white
man had ever ascended." Does any place exist until it has
been recorded by man? The sense of eager discovery is strong
in this portion of the journals. The weather is pleasant, geese
are flying; there are signs of Indians but no Indians, save a
dead woman on a scaffold, deposited with her dog beside her;
there are signs of bear; the prairie hens are mating — "the note
of the male, is kuck, kuck, kuck, coo, coo, coo"; buffalo,
wolves, deer, elk, antelope, beaver are in evidence. Lewis becomes increasingly lyric and anxious. On May 9: "I begin
to feel extreemly anxious to get in view of the rocky mountains." On May 26: "I beheld the Rocky Mountains for the
first time . . . [and] while I viewed these mountains I felt a
secret pleasure in finding myself so near the head of the heretofore conceived boundless Missouri." Later he writes: "the
river bottoms form one emence garden of roses, now in full
bloe," and in mid-June at the Great Falls of the Missouri,
it is Lewis who writes: "I wished for the pencil of Salvator
Rosa [*a Titian*] or the pen of Thompson, that I might be en-
abled to give to the enlightened world some just idea of this
truly magnifficent and sublimely grand object." It is noteworthy that Lewis was off exploring the Falls by himself when
he waxed so poetic. It is typical of him that after penning a
lengthy description he was chased into the water by a bear.
Later in the day, three buffalo ran full speed toward him;
finally, walking back the twelve miles to the rest of the party,
he reflects: "the succession of curious adventures wore the
impression on my mind of inchantment; at sometimes for a
moment I thought it might be a dream, but the prickly pears
which pierced my feet very severely once in a while, particularly after it grew dark, convinced me that I was really
awake." The point is that it was a long way from James Thomson to prickly pears, and, of course, Thomson's tropes
wouldn't serve any more.

Lewis' romantic passages give an entirely artificial picture of what was actually happening on this part of the journey. One needs in reading the contrast of the more matter-of-

fact Clark. In reality, the hardships had increased. There were ticks, mosquitoes, and rattlesnakes. The river banks fell in suddenly, nearly swamping the boats. Heavy head winds almost brought catastrophe. A violent hailstorm mauled the men, even knocking them down. Boats and equipment had to be portaged around the Falls, a labor of over three weeks, marked by the exhaustion of the supply of whiskey on July 4 — "The party amused themselves danceing untill late when a shower of rain broke up the amusement, all lively and Chearfull." Reality always dominated in the West. The concept of a folding boat, so brilliant in the East, had to be abandoned when the reassembled iron boat leaked. To anticipate history, two streams were discovered and named Wisdom and Philanthropy, in honor of the cardinal virtues of Jefferson; fact has more recently renamed the streams Big Hole and Stinking Water. But finally, on August 12, the end of the Missouri was reached, a stream which one of the men could straddle, "bestride the mighty & heretofore deemed endless Missouri." It was a moment of triumph, but, as Lewis continues the passage, "after refreshing ourselves we proceeded on to the top of the dividing ridge from which I discovered immence ranges of high mountains still to the West of us with their tops partially covered with snow." It was a disheartening view.

The expedition shifts into another key. The reader of the journals is carried on into the sober maturity of the men. It was soon clear that there was no easy water route to the coast. The long search for the Passage to India had ended in the "immense ranges of high mountains still to the West." The wild game on which they survived disappeared in the barren mountains. The dehydrated "portable" soup was used up. The boats were exchanged for twenty-nine horses purchased from the Shoshonis, horses to "Eate if necessary." The painful trip down the Lolo trail and then in dugouts down the Snake and Columbia rivers is narrated by Clark alone. No doubt Lewis kept a journal which has been lost, but it is as if he could not bear to record the hungry and ugly trip. Clark's field-note version of September 24 is succinct and clear: "Capt Lewis sick   all Complain of a *Lax* & heaviness at the stomack, I gave rushes Pills to several." On October 18 the men exchanged bells, thimbles, knitting pins, brass wire, and a few beads for forty dogs, on which they survived. The passages of late October, dealing with the narrows of the Columbia, are nightmarish. It is typical of the trip that on November 7, when Clark wrote *"Ocian in view*! O! the joy," he did not see the ocean at all. The other exclamations which follow it temper the accomplishment: "O! how disagreeable is our Situation dureing this dreadfull weather." "The winds violent   Trees falling in every derection, whorl winds, with gusts of rain Hail & Thunder, this kind of weather lasted all day. Certainly one of the worst days that ever was!" Christmas Day was the nadir. "Our Diner to day consisted of pore Elk boiled, spilt [spoiled] fish & some roots, a bad Christmass diner."

Unlike Clark, Lewis has not quite yet lost his *savoir-faire*. When he resumes his journal on January 1, 1806, it is to write: "our repast of this day tho' better than that of Christmass, consisted principally in the anticipation of the 1st day of January 1807, when in the bosom of our friends we hope to participate in the mirth and hilarity of the day, and when with the zest given by the recollection of the present, we shall completely, both mentally and corporally, enjoy the repast which the hand of civilization has prepared for us." That homesick hope sustained them all through the constant winter rains at Fort Clatsop and then in the weary retracing of the rivers, back to the horses for the passage over the mountains. The strain begins to tell on Lewis, and we remark his honesty in recording it. When one of the men carelessly let the horses wander off, Lewis wrote, "this in addition to the other difficulties under which I laboured was truly provoking. I repremanded him more severely for this piece of negligence than had been usual with me." Two days later he caught a thieving Indian and "gave him several severe blows." In May a crisis arose: "while at dinner an indian fellow verry imper-

tinently threw a poor half starved puppy nearly into my plait
by way of derision for our eating dogs and laughed very
heartily at his own impertinence; I was so provoked at his
insolence that I caught the puppy and th[r]ew it with great
violence at him and stru[c]k him in the breast and face, siezed
my tomahawk and shewed him by signs if he repeated his
insolence I would tommahawk him, the fellow withdrew apparently much mortifyed and I continued my repast *on dog*
without further molestation." No other narrative device could
be as clear as Lewis' own, so personal that we can hear his
voice today.

But then, once at the mountains, there was too much snow
to continue:"that icy barier which seperates me from my
friends and Country, from all which makes life esteemable."
Lewis ends the passage with an exquisite touch: " —patience, patience." They delayed until June, until the Indians
said it was safe. Suddenly, all the danger was past: "our party
seem much elated with the idea of moving on towards their
friends and country, they all seem allirt in their movements
today; they have every thing in readiness for a move."

The repassage of the mountains, though dangerous enough,
was easier than anticipated, and the expedition entered a final stage. The captains separated, Clark to strike east from
Three Forks to the Yellowstone River and thence downstream; Lewis to cut directly across to the Great Falls and
on to explore an alternative route to the Pacific, Marias River,
which had seemed in 1805 as large as the Missouri itself. The
journals of the men, now written without recourse to the
thoughts of each other, are strikingly different.

Clark, on his own, is all Clark. I order, I observed, I shot,
I halted, I inclined, I sent, I order — the pronoun is repeated
seven times in the page-long passage for July 4. It is all very
military and efficient. His party arose early; if they delayed
to make canoe paddles, it was still to depart at 7:00; if the
horses were scattered they were rounded up by 8:00; if at
9:00, it was "much later than common." Clark pushed his
horses hard, and when they were lame, he had "Mockersons"

made of green buffalo skin so the horses could continue. Charbonneau's horse, chasing a buffalo, stepped into a hole and
threw Charbonneau, who was "a good deel brused on his hip
sholder & face. after brackfast I proceeded on as usial," wrote
Clark. Gibson was wounded, falling on a sharp point of a
tree; "time is pracious," wrote Clark, and built a litter for Gibson. He stopped, it would seem, only long enough to cut his
name in the rock of Pompey's Pillar, and then, two days later, "I marked my name with red paint on a cotton tree near
my camp, and Set out at an early hour." He arrived at the
rendezvous nine days before Lewis. As readers, we sorely
miss his partner.

Lewis, on his own, had two strokes of bad luck, both nearly
fatal, one tragic, one farcical. On the afternoon of Saturday,
July 26, 1806, Lewis and his party of six on horseback in the
vicinity of Marias River stumbled on a hunting party of eight
Piegans, members of the Blackfoot tribe. Lewis was not sufficiently wary. He made camp with the Indians, distributed
a medal, a flag, and a handkerchief, and at 11:30 that night,
after setting Joseph Fields on watch, he "feel into a profound
sleep." Fields stayed awake, but he was careless. He put his
gun down behind him. When Lewis was awakened at daybreak, the Piegans were in the act of stealing four guns —
Lewis' included. It was Reuben Fields who gave chase and
seized the guns and "stabed the indian to the heart with his
knife." The Piegans next tried to run off the horses. Lewis
pursued on foot, ran till he was out of breath, shouted a warn-
ing, and then with his recovered rifle aimed at one man and
"shot him through the belly." Even with this, Lewis bum-
bled. Before expiring, the Indian fired back, just missing. As
Lewis wrote later, "being bearheaded I felt the wind of his
bullet very distinctly." Lewis and his men rode hard out of
the vicinity. It had been an exciting day, and it was narrated
by Lewis in great detail, without apology, sparing nothing
concerning his own ineptitudes.

Two weeks later, Monday, August 11, Lewis pushed to arrive at certain burned hills, the northernmost point of the

Missouri, in order to make a meridian reading of latitude. He arrived too late (of course) for the reading, and thus went off with Pierre Cruzatte after elk on a sand bar of thick willows. Apparently Cruzatte, nearsighted and with vision in only one eye, shot at what he thought was an elk, but it turned out to be Lewis, dressed in brown leather — shot him in the left thigh (Ordway is clearer: "his buttock"), the ball passing through. "Damn you, you have shot me," Lewis called out, and the direct quotation is refreshing. Cruzatte, apparently appalled at what he had done, did not answer. Lewis, therefore, presumed he had been shot by an Indian. He *ran* to the boat for help, sent the men on to defend Cruzatte, and with pistol, rifle, and air rifle beside him determined "to sell my life as deerly as possible." Alas, it was only Cruzatte, and one can imagine Captain Clark's countenance when he heard the story from Lewis three days later. Lewis was badly wounded and would not be able to walk for about three weeks. The meeting with Clark on August 12 is Lewis' last entry in the journal. His close is typical and heart-warming: "as wrighting in my present situation is extreemly painfull to me I shall desist untill I recover and leave to my fri[e]nd Capt. C. the continuation of our journal. however I must notice a singular Cherry which is found on the Missouri in the bottom lands about the beaver bends and some little distance below the white earth river" and so on, for another hundred words of description, unconsciously poetic.

Clark concludes the journals swiftly, as swiftly as the party moved downstream. They coasted down from the Little Missouri River on August 13 to Fort Belle Fontaine near St. Louis on September 22. The homecoming was marked by buying whiskey on September 6 from a trading boat of Chouteau and then "several of the party exchanged leather for linen Shirts." On September 20 "we saw some cows on the bank which was a joyfull Sight to the party and caused a Shout to be raised for joy." That night, at the village of La Charette, a citizen charged them $8 cash for two gallons of whiskey, "an imposition on the part of the citizen," Clark adds. Linen shirts, cows, and a wily citizen — they were home indeed.

They were home, and the carefully guarded journals with their treasures of discovery were safe. A new world was in their pockets, and the old world eagerly awaited the publication of the journals — or so one would think. In actual fact, the world hardly seemed to care. Lewis and Clark went east and were lionized for a time as Western curiosities. In 1807 Lewis issued a prospectus announcing the future publication of the official journals, but the East read Gass's cheap (in both senses of the word) and brief version of the expedition and was satisfied. Lewis' death in 1809 left the duty of publication to Clark, and the unschooled Clark sensibly found a literary man to edit the collective journals. The publication of the Biddle edition — finally, in 1814 — provided a third and curious version of the journals of Lewis and Clark.

From Clark's point of view, Nicholas Biddle was an excellent choice. He was educated (Princeton); he was literate (an editor of *Port Folio*); he was only twenty-four and energetic to make a name for himself; he was wealthy and consequently had helpful Philadelphia connections, to say nothing of the requisite leisure for an onerous task. Clark supplied Biddle with the journals (including that of Ordway) and with the person of George Shannon, a private on the expedition. He answered Biddle's questions orally or by letter — and waited for his book to appear.

From another point of view, Clark's choice of Biddle was not much better than Gass's choice of McKeehan as his editor, who had produced such a flat and ordinary book. Nicholas Biddle worked for a year on the journals and then quit. In that year he campaigned for the lower house of the state legislature, won, and spent the winter in an initial defense of the Bank of the United States. In the same year, he fell in love with his future wife and spent uncounted hours wooing Jane Craig and writing limpid billet-doux to her mother, the rich, cultivated, cosmopolitan widow Margaret Craig (with whom Biddle conferred on his editing problems). He was a busy, climbing young man.[12]

In addition, one might say that Biddle's education had thoroughly *un*fitted him for the work he attempted. At Princeton he was nicknamed "Grammaticus," "possibly as a semi-ironic commentary upon his precocious learning and his grave and pedagogic manner."[13] He wrote defenses of Federalism and on "The Evils of Intemperance and the Joys of Drinking Wine." In Philadelphia he fell under the sway of Joseph Dennie, who accustomed Biddle to essays satirizing tea parties or burlesquing literary criticism, and instilled in him a "taste for elegant literature,"[14] to quote Biddle's eulogy of Dennie. In Europe on the Grand Tour, Biddle imbibed a classicism and cosmopolitanism such that he could translate Greek or French poetry and discourse on Machiavelli. He was, in short, a litterateur, trained in manners and mannerisms, fitted to edit the *Port Folio* (after Dennie's demise in drink), that minor literary journal of a minor literary period.

Biddle, soon too busy to finish the editing of the journals, turned the work over to Paul Allen, an editorial assistant on the *Port Folio*; he did we don't know how much additional writing before publication,[15] but *his* approach can be judged by his letter to Jefferson requesting a biographical sketch of Lewis to preface the journals:"I wish very much to enliven the dulness of the Narrative by something more popular splendid & attractive. The publick taste has from a variety of adventious causes been gorged to repletion on fanciful viands & the most nutritive & invigorating aliments will not be relished unless seasoned with Something of that character. Bi-

[12] All details on Biddle are from Thomas Payne Govan, *Nicholas Biddle, Nationalist and Public Banker, 1786–1844* (Chicago: University of Chicago Press, 1959), *passim*.

[13] *Ibid.*, p. 5.

[14] Quoted in *ibid.*, p. 39.

[15] See the discussion by Jackson, p. 585n.

ography partakes to a certain extent of this quality."[16] So, between them, Biddle and Allen, fitting the West to the refined tastes of the East, managed to ruin the journals of Lewis and Clark.

The Biddle version cut the manuscript from 900,000 words to 370,000 words.[17] Roughly a third of the material, which Clark called the "cientific part," was omitted because it was reserved for the naturalist Dr. Benjamin Smith Barton (who died before he could work on his project). The other third was a matter of condensing the duplicate journals of a part of the trip (April-August, 1805) and a general tightening-up of the narrative, changing, as Thwaites put it, a "mass of heterogeneous data into a readable paraphrase."[18] After acknowledging the really great editorial skill of Biddle in doing just that, I must censure him on both counts of omission.

The "cientific part" of the journals was the essence of them. Lewis and Clark made every effort to identify and describe the animals, birds, fish, and reptiles which they encountered. They wrote, for example, "the first detailed descriptions of the grizzly bear, the mule deer, the pronghorn antelope, the Columbian whitetail deer, the Columbian blacktail deer, the kit fox, the Mountain beaver, the prairie dog, the Columbian ground squirrel, the bushytail woodrat, the eastern woodrat, the whitetail jackrabbit, the Oregon bobcat, and Douglas' squirrel."[19] They described twenty-two new birds, six fish, five reptiles, and four amphibians.[20] They mapped and described thousands of miles of rivers. They wrote about plants and minerals and climate and Indians. Some of this ma-

[16] *Ibid.*, p. 586.

[17] Thwaites's calculations, I, xliv–xlv.

[18] *Ibid.*, p. xlv.

[19] Raymond Darwin Burroughs, *The Natural History of the Lewis and Clark Expedition* (East Lansing: Michigan State University Press, 1961), p. vii.

[20] *Ibid.*, p. viii. Burroughs, p. 283, totals for the first time the game killed for food by the expedition: 1,001 deer, 375 elk, 227 bison, 66 bears, 190 dogs (purchased from the Indians), etc. It is a fantastic slaughter.

terial is in Biddle, but most of it is not, and that is the point: Lewis and Clark spent their time assiduously making observations, taking measurements, collecting specimens, and spelling out the natural history of half a continent. To omit this is to distort. The labored descriptions of strange animals, the groping for terms of comparison, the movement and the sounds and the colors, so patiently and precisely detailed — these are the life of the narrative, not the tedium.

Biddle's paraphrase and condensing of the journals is an even greater error. Refer back to the record of October 1, 1804, quoted previously. This is Biddle's version: "On the opposite shore, we saw a house among the willows and a boy, to whom we called, and brought him on board. He proved to be a young Frenchman in the employ of a Mr. Valle a trader, who is now here pursuing his commerce with the Sioux." Biddle has Mr. Valle visit with Lewis and Clark the next morning, omitting the night's gossip over the campfire in favor of a summary the next day. Where Clark said, "The black mountains he Says is verry high, and Some parts of it has Snow on it in the Summer," Biddle changes to "The Black mountains he observes are very high, covered with great quantities of pine, and in some parts the snow remains during the summer," a version decidedly smoother, but weakened in the process of change. Biddle has no sense of tone. In addition, he left out virtually all personal references. He changed the first person singular to the first person plural; when the men moved separately, he referred to them as "captain Clark" or "captain Lewis," not as "I." He gained in this way a certain coherence, but he lost a great deal of literary force. The reading of the journals presented here depends on the interplay of personality — on style: the unconscious, naive, revealing word choice of two different men. Biddle, however, imposes himself between the men and their reader, leveling, smoothing out differences. The result can be termed either "readable paraphrase" or emasculation.

Biddle's style is, by contrast with that of Lewis and Clark, learned and artificial, with no relation to the materials with

which he dealt. The matter has been studied in detail by
Professor Elijah Harry Criswell, who summarizes thus: "Biddle had changed and 'improved' the wording of the explorers throughout, thus effectively removing most of the distinctive linguistic and stylistic interest of their work." [21] Criswell's
lexicon lists 1,859 words used by Lewis and Clark for the first
time in America: word coinages, first usages of distinctively
American terms, and so on, even to some peculiarities stem-
ming directly from American backwoods usage of Middle
English. Criswell calls Lewis and Clark linguistic pioneers,
but Biddle changed the language to fit Philadelphia, Joseph
Dennie, and his future mother-in-law. It would not be a matter to get excited about, if the Biddle version had died; but
with the exception of Thwaites's original journals in 1904 and
DeVoto's condensation of the journals in 1953, the world knew
of the expedition only through Biddle's rose-colored glasses.[22]

Biddle's spelling corrections in one fell swoop destroy the
character of the men. Tied to his elevated style and gentility,
he has formalized, stiffened, and killed the journals as literature. Demonstrations are in order. Biddle wrote, "the mosquitoes and ticks are exceedingly troublesome"; but Clark
had written, "The Ticks & Musquiters are verry troublesome,"
a much more natural expression. Biddle wrote, "a plain extended itself as far as the eye could discern" where Clark had
used simpler terms: "the Countrey is leavel & open as far as
can be Seen." Biddle wrote, "the evening was closed by a
dance," but Clark had been more detailed: "the evening was
closed with an extra gill of whiskey and a Dance untill 11
oClock." Biddle wrote of the men, "several had their feet
frostbitten," but Clark had written, "my Servents feet also
frosted & his P——s a little." On a boat accident, Biddle
wrote, "Such was the confusion on board, and the waves ran

[21] Elijah H. Criswell, *Lewis and Clark: Linguistic Pioneers* (Columbia: University of Missouri, 1940), p. xi.

[22] In print today are the Thwaites edition and DeVoto. The paperback
editions — Lippincott and Dover — are Biddle. Heritage Press has issued an illustrated edition of the journals — Biddle once again.

so high, that it was half a minute before she righted, and then nearly full of water." But Lewis had been excitingly clear: "the perogue then wrighted but had filled within an inch of the gunwals; Charbono still crying to his god for mercy, had not yet recollected the rudder, nor could the repeated orders of the Bowsman, Cruzat, bring him to his recollection untill he threatend to shoot him instantly if he did not take hold of the rudder and do his duty." Biddle lists the English words learned by the coast Indians as "musket, powder, shot, knife, file, heave the lead, damned rascal, and other phrases of that description"; but Lewis' list included "sun of a bitch," which Clark spelled "*Sun of a pitch*." One could cite a thousand bowdlerizations and "improvements" by Biddle.

Biddle's omissions are equally bad. The several courts-martial and lashings are reduced in Biddle to one occasion: "After dinner we stopped on a sandbar, and executed the sentence of a court martial which inflicted corporal punishment on one of the soldiers." He generalizes; the omissions falsify. When Clark writes, "I felt My Self warm & Spoke in verry positive terms," Biddle says nothing. When Clark writes "O! how disagreeable my situation," Biddle says nothing — though Lewis' wrath while eating dog, cited above, is given in detail. Biddle is not squeamish; he relates incidents of sexual intercourse and venereal diseases, though without naming names. Biddle leaves out some of the accidents — Lewis' fall from a horse and his fall into the river. He leaves out some of the whiskey (April 26, 1805, for example) and does not mention the wily citizen of September 20, 1806. He leaves out some of Lewis' reflections. The fine departure from Fort Mandan — "we were now about to penetrate a country at least two thousand miles in width, on which the foot of civilized man had never trodden" — is a blank in Biddle. He leaves out McNeal's straddling of the Missouri River. He leaves out the touching and revealing comments Lewis makes on his thirty-first birthday, August 18, 1805. He glosses over, smoothes out, leaves out, and so warps the journals to his own "refined" taste.

Biddle's additions are stylized, rhetorical fluff. Lewis' description of the Great Falls was pompous enough, but Biddle outdoes him: "The scene which it presented was indeed singularly beautiful, since without any of the wild irregular sublimity of the lower falls, it combined all the regular elegances which the fancy of a painter would select to form a beautiful waterfall. The eye had scarcely been regaled with this charming prospect, when at the distance of half a mile captain Lewis observed another of a similar kind: to this he immediately hastened." Nor could he neglect his own classical learning. Of an Arikara legend of dead lovers, Biddle says, "Their history would adorn the metamorphoses of Ovid." When he describes a Buffalo dance, curiously sexual and not found in the original journals, he does this in Latin. Circumlocution and elevated diction are consistent faults of Biddle on every page. Another addition is the more frequent references to Sacajawea, whom Biddle idolizes, thus starting that warping of the history of the expedition with its erroneous sequel of Sacajawea, the mistress of Clark or the savior of the expedition, which preoccupies authors to the present day.

To cage and to tame, like the "burrowing squirrel" or prairie dog brought from West to East, is to destroy. The literary qualities of the Lewis and Clark journals should not be mangled by paraphrase or condensation. The *Journals* are in eight volumes, but omitting the one of maps, the one of letters and the journals of Floyd and Whitehouse, and another of summary observations, the pith of the original journals is in a readable form. These are the raw materials of history, but they can be avoided. The alternatives are Nicholas Biddle or Bernard DeVoto (who digests to about half the original length, supplying italicized connective passages, but carefully observing the original spelling) or John Bakeless (whose *Lewis and Clark* [1947] is a learned and readable history) or Vardis Fisher (whose *Tale of Valor* [1958] is probably the best fictional treatment of the expedition). In each interpretation, however, the reader loses the sense of immediacy which only the original journal can provide.

Slowly and patiently working his way through the disordered firsthand impressions, the reader begins to feel a sense of unlimited space and time. The seasons wheel and merge — "here we have summer spring and winter within the short space of 15 or 20 miles." The broad rivers shrink to tiny trickles and expand again to the "ocian." Like poor Shannon, so far astray he did not hear the sound of the tin trumpets, the reader roams in Eden, oblivious to the sound of time.

Here is natural man, hauling a canoe up a river (more rock than water) by his brute force, and dancing in the evening to Cruzatte's violin. Here is the noble savage, eagerly chewing the raw entrails of a deer, or, like Sacajawea's babe, listening at night to the rutting calls of buffalo. Here is an anonymous soldier visiting a Mandan medicine dance and being staggered by the present of four girls. Here is Clark's black servant York, dancing on his head to entertain the Indians. Here is the anxious, bumbling Lewis learning just short of the cost of his life to respect a certain animal: "I must confess that I do not like the gentleman and had reather fight two Indians than one bear." And it is Lewis who acknowledges in passing the order of providence, but never prays, never glorifies a god, never relies on anyone but his confrere Clark. Modestly warm to each other, distant and formal physically, bowing to each other's superior skill whether it was in spelling or hunting, concerned for each other when separated, Lewis and Clark, "my worthy friend and companion," not interchangeable but separate entities in an unbelievably working relationship — these are made clearest of all in the changes of authorship of the journals. One thinks of Whitman's stumbling and beautiful lines in "Pioneers! O Pioneers!":

> O you youths, Western youths,
> So impatient, full of action, full of manly pride
> and friendship.

Our American literary tastes today are for the rough, realistic base — the naive man awkwardly recording the terror and wonder of his existence. We look for purity of impression, for intensity — not cold dispassion, not random passion, but the individual in the tension of his awareness of his existence in a fathomless universe. Such terms suggest the literary qualities of the Lewis and Clark journals: man and his materials — the fiddle, the tin trumpet, the sword, the folding boat, the portable soup, the air gun, the medicinal mercury, the portable desk — symbols of the conditions for the survival of man on the Western frontier.

3

THE EARLY NOVELISTS:
Timothy Flint and James Hall

The first major work of fiction about the West was written by a hypochondriac minister who never came within twenty-five miles of the eastern edge of the vast country he wrote about, and it is interesting to watch his writing grow progressively worse as he moves farther away from his own experiences. For it is a simple axiom of good writing that fiction must follow fact, and *Francis Berrian, or The Mexican Patriot* (1826), ostensibly Western in origin, actually very Eastern in derivation, is highly predictive of the thousands of fictional failures which followed the romantic pattern set up by this Chateaubriand-Flint.

The Reverend Timothy Flint, novelist, was a contradiction in terms; perhaps he should never have been a clergyman. But he came from a family of Congregational deacons from North Reading, Massachusetts, and went naturally from Harvard, graduating in 1800, to his ordination in 1802 into the church at Lunenberg, a parish attached to the town of Fitchburg, Massachusetts. There his troubles began. He leaned toward Unitarianism, but his parish was Trinitarian. He was a Federalist, but his parish was democratic. His salary was small, but his family grew large. "Starvation and insult exhausted my health," he wrote; he became, as he said, "slavish through fear of offending," and he appears to have retreated to the romances of Imlay and Chateaubriand as an escape from his ministerial vexations.[1] When the parish refused his bid in 1814 for an increase in salary, Flint resigned and requested of the Missionary Society of Connecticut a Western mission, so that he might find a milder, beneficial climate and so that he might establish a religious publication (literary aspirations, indeed). Flint's *Recollections of the Last Ten Years* (1826) begins with the October, 1815, departure with wife and three children from New England.

Those ten years constitute Flint's basic Western experience, and since he set himself up as such an authority on the West, his peregrinations — journeys from one misfortune to another — should be noted. The Flints went by coach from New England to Pittsburgh and by flatboat down the Ohio River to Cincinnati, to spend the winter there with relatives. In the early spring of 1816, Timothy made a solitary circuit on horseback to Lexington, Kentucky. Then the Flints resumed the boat trip down the Ohio to Cairo, Illinois, and north on the Mississippi River to St. Louis. Flint settled that autumn on invitation at St. Charles, forty miles up the Missouri River from St. Louis; he worked there for two years as a missionary while his wife conducted a school for young girls. Flint traveled in the area, preaching where he could, but was so severe on sinners that he made himself highly unpopular. A fellow missionary, Salmon Giddings, wrote to the Missionary Society that Flint "is a Speculator, Avaricious, Immoral and of course, not a Christian,"[2] and poor Flint gracefully re-

---

[1] John Ervin Kirkpatrick, *Timothy Flint* (Cleveland: Arthur H. Clark, 1911), p. 43. This is virtually the only biographical source aside from Flint's own *Recollections*, for Flint family papers were laid waste by a cyclone in Arkansas, by the Union Army in Alexandria, and by the Galveston flood. Nothing is added in James K. Folsom, *Timothy Flint* (New York: Twayne Publishers, 1965), pp. 17–47.

[2] *Ibid.*, p. 114.

signed, claiming that the country wasn't ready for him. ("When I brought terror into their billiard-rooms, and a blush into their faces at beholding their likeness depicted with independence and fidelity of intention at least, they began to talk of starving me out." [3]) He resigned in June, 1818, promptly fell deathly ill, and could not leave St. Charles until April, 1819. He went by flatboat down the Mississippi to the Arkansas River and fifty miles up that river to Arkansas Post. His efforts to establish a mission there failed; the population was French; his command of that language was limited, and he could not make an impression on the "rough and untamed" [4] people. In October, 1819, he headed back north, but was brought to a halt for the winter at New Madrid, Missouri, moving on the next spring to the town of Jackson, Missouri ("my time passed more devoid of interest, or of attachment, or comfort, or utility, than in any other part of the country"), for the year 1820-21. The people of Jackson could not or would not (as Flint felt) pay him a living salary, and Flint went back to St. Charles in October, determined to make his way as a farmer. The whole family fell promptly ill with the ague, and the Missionary Society of Connecticut did not respond to his plea for help.

A year later, October, 1822, rescued financially by Eastern friends, the Flints headed home — via New Orleans. But sunshine and good health encouraged them to stay in Louisiana. Flint went in 1823 to take charge of a seminary at Covington, across Lake Ponchartrain, but, as one critic says, "Health failed, as usual, and he returned to New Orleans in the autumn." [5] He tried one more position in 1823, this time at a seminary at Alexandria, Louisiana, two hundred miles northwest on the Red River. Here at last he found a congenial

[3] *Ibid.*, p. 293.
[4] Timothy Flint, *Recollections of the Last Ten Years*, C. Hartley Grattan, ed. (New York: Knopf, 1932), p. 260. Future quotations from this text are not footnoted.
[5] William H. Venable, *Beginnings of Literary Culture in the Ohio Valley* (Cincinnati: R. Clarke, 1891), p. 345.

ministry and might have stayed on, but, as Flint himself records it, "I was then seized with a bilious complaint, accompanied with spasm, which confined me to my bed. All the
aids of medicine were unavailing." A winter trip in January,
1825 (of which more later), was not helpful. Flint went alone
back north by steamboat to Wheeling and on to Massachusetts by way of the National Road, "come home," he said,
"to die."

For all the personal vicissitudes and failures, Flint had
been, unaware, in a unique position to study the crude society of the lower Mississippi valley, and there would be no
equivalent observer until Mark Twain began piloting in 1857.
Apparently prompted by the previous inquiries of a Salem,
Massachusetts, cousin and by "the wish of such friends, that
I should tell the story of what I have seen and suffered,"
Flint wrote in the summer and fall of 1825 the series of letters
which were to be his *Recollections* and published it at Boston
in 1826. This excellent work is not, by our definition, Western.
Flint, family-bound, could not go much beyond the roughly
civilized line of the Mississippi River. But this work, with its
careful reportage and literary aspiration, is the base for the
later fiction.

With no little skill Flint reorganized his erratic travels
onto a progressive geographical line, beginning in New England, moving to Pittsburgh, Cincinnati, and Lexington, the
main stops in the Ohio valley; then on to St. Louis, St. Charles,
Jackson, and New Madrid, his Missouri stops; then to Arkansas and Louisiana, ending with a short summary of the return
trip. At each stop, he tells enough personal history to account
for his presence (detailing each illness), but then goes beyond personality to a more or less objective description of the
land and its people. But Flint's personal problems, his constant retreat from reality, inhibit the factual record. His schiz-
ophrenia was aggravated by the failures which are easily
traced in his own *Recollections.*

As a minister he began auspiciously enough on the road
to Pittsburgh, trying to reform the drovers. "I often dropped

among them, as by accident, that impressive tract, the
'Swearer's Prayer.'" He was pleased with the results, yet he
soon discovered "the prevailing vices of the West — gambling and intemperance." When he tried reform he found that
the young men "spoke of their failing with the tone of peni-
tents, who confess, deplore, but mean to sin again." Once
across the Mississippi he found he had indeed traveled "beyond the Sabbath." Of his fellow preachers, itinerants like
himself, he said, "I did not hear one who approached mediocrity" (and in fiction he would sketch in the Reverend Thomas S——, an appallingly avaricious character). Throughout
his travels he seemed to labor in a moral wilderness, and
he was frank to acknowledge that he had been misled by
his imagination. Enlarging on the point, he found that the
whole rush of emigrants was motivated in part by what he
termed a desire for poetry:

Very few, except the Germans, emigrate simply to find better and
cheaper lands. The notion of new and more beautiful woods and
streams, of a milder climate, deer, fish, fowl, game, and all those
delightful images of enjoyment, that so readily associate with the
idea of the wild and boundless license of new regions; all that restless hope of finding in a new country, and in new views and com-
binations of things, something that we crave but have not, — I
am ready to believe, from my own experience, and from what I
have seen in the case of others, that this influence of imagination
has no inconsiderable agency in producing emigration.

The inevitable then happens:

A few weeks' familiar acquaintance with the scene dispels the
charms and the illusions of the imagination. The earth, the water,
and the wood of these distant lands, are found to be the same well
known realities of his own country. . . . Every thing visionary
and unreal gradually gives way to truth and reality.

Flint was quite ready to lead an Arcadian life on the plains —
until he saw "the wild and savage nature" in the West which
had etched gloom on the faces of Indians. But people are
drawn on by a will-o'-the-wisp. At one time the Mississippi
had been the border, the "'ultima Thule' — a limit almost to
the range of thought." Now, he wrote,

Nothing can or will limit the immigration westward, but the Western Ocean. Alas! for the moving generation of the day, when the
tide of advancing backwoodsmen shall have met the surge of the
Pacific. They may then set them down and weep for other worlds.

With that haunting picture, Flint retreated from the frontier to the culture of Louisiana and finally to the artifice of
fiction.

The *Recollections* are, however, a reasonably realistic history. Just how realistic we know through the testimony of a
noted contemporary, James Kirke Paulding, who borrowed
generously from Flint in writing his own novel *Westward Ho!*
(1832) and who in 1842 retraced Flint's Mississippi River travels. Paulding's marginal notations in Flint's *A Condensed Geography and History of the Western States* (1828)
show clearly the accuracy of Flint's work.[6] Flint generalizes
about the West far beyond the basis of his actual experience,
but on the whole the *Recollections* are a satisfying social history. But in search of literature we ask of a writer that he go
beyond the level of casual reportage, that he give shape to
and vivify his material in the form of fiction, and it is just
here that Flint begins to fail.

Throughout the *Recollections* there is a story-telling tendency. From the moment Flint reached the Mississippi River
in the spring of 1816 he found everything "novel and fresh,"
for as yet "the illusion had not given place to the sad reality."
He was particularly struck by his western boatmen, who, after the labor of cordelling the boat upriver by day, at night
would tell each other tales of their western experiences:
"These stories, told by the boatmen stretched at the foot of
a tree, just below which was the boat, and the wave of the
Mississippi, and interlarded with the jargon of their peculiar
phrase, or perhaps interrupted by the droll comment, or the
incredulous questioning of the rest, had often to me no small
degree of interest; and tricked out in the dress of modern description, would have made very tolerable romances." Al-

[6] Arlin Turner, "James K. Paulding and Timothy Flint," *Mississippi
Valley Historical Review*, XXXIV (June, 1947), 105–111.

though we might be suspicious of that "tricked out in the dress of modern description," we are alerted because Flint is not superior to dialect, alerted because he was conscious of a relation between the people and their land. But if his original journals recorded such talk, the manuscripts were blown away later in an Arkansas cyclone.

The violent country, the violent people, a writer of some skill, and on-the-spot experiences — thus we turn to Flint's fiction. We will find to our vast disappointment that his fiction represents an escape from the West, not at all that interpretation of the West for which we seek. His retreat back into illusion is an avoiding of the problem, but it is typical of the West-to-East pattern in American literary history. Flint's first novel traces the stages of that knowing retreat from experience into the realm of fantasy.

We must recall the situation of Flint in the fall of 1824. He is in his second year in charge of a "college" and church (Presbyterian) at Alexandria, Louisiana. Knowing Flint, we know he will fall sick. He tells his own story in the *Recollections*:

In October of the last year, we resumed our laborious duties in the seminary. I had my son and another young man under a particular course of personal instruction. I had boarders, a numerous school, preached after a sort and as I could, and was trying to digest this work. A few weeks of this overplied exertion began to make me feel the illness, which brought me to your country. I struggled to vanquish it, by resolution and exercise. . . . The middle of January, I was just able, with assistance, to mount on horse back. Accompanied by my friend, Judge Bullard . . . I commenced a journey to Natchitoches and the interior beyond for my health.

Out of this trip grew *Francis Berrian*, and since Berrian was modeled on Judge Bullard, a word concerning the judge is necessary.

Henry Adams Bullard was then, in 1824, thirty-six; when he was twenty-four, in Philadelphia (after his degree from Harvard in 1807 and after the study of law), he had fallen in with the Mexican revolutionary José Alvarez de Toledo, who was planning a private expeditionary force into Texas. Bullard and Alvarez spent the winter of 1812-13 recruiting personnel in Nashville, and in the spring of 1813 moved to Natchitoches, Louisiana, and sometime later joined the Army of the North (the private army of Jose Bernardo Maximiliano Gutierrez de Lara and the former American army officer Augustus Gagee), which had entered Spanish Texas in August, 1812, and in 1813 seized San Antonio in the Battle of Rosalis. This was, of course, a premature "revolution," which ended in August, 1813, when Spain sent 3,000 troops up from Mexico to rout these privateers. Bullard's Mexican adventure was short: he arrived in time for the battle and a perilous retreat to Natchitoches. There he was to settle down, to marry, and to become a state district judge, his adventures at an end.[7]

Bullard by 1824 was a substantial, affluent gentleman; his trip to Natchitoches was a sentimental return to the romantic events of his youth, and of course he regaled Flint with stories of his past. They stayed two weeks in Natchitoches, and Flint received "daily invitations to entertainments by the hospitable citizens," a mixture of Spanish, French, and Americans. (While there, Flint even accompanied a French murderer to the gallows — an indication of the strangeness of the life he was meeting.) From Natchitoches, they made "an excursion towards the Spanish frontier" — an odd phrase for Flint to use, since Mexico had been free from Spain since 1821. His nearest approach to the West (referring back to my initial distinction) was still twenty-five miles away from the dividing line of the Sabine River, stopping at Cantonment Jessup (now the town of Fort Jessup, Louisiana), where two companies of soldiers occupied the farthest southwesterly army post in the United States. Flint's actual Western experiences, in other words, take him up to only page 40 of

[7] Dora J. Bonquois, "The Career of Henry Adams Bullard, Louisiana Jurist, Legislator, and Educator," *Louisiana Historical Quarterly*, XXIII (October, 1940), 995–1106.

Francis Berrian — and the rest is fabrication. But he was determined to write about the experiences of his friend Bullard; he collected background materials — and unfortunately had to return to Alexandria, too sick even to ride a horse. An "exhausted invalid," all he could do was return to the East with the hope that he would be buried by the grave of his parents.

Flint returned east in April, 1825, but he did not die. With a miraculous recovery and an inexplicable speed, he published both the *Recollections* and *Francis Berrian* the following year. *Francis Berrian* is important to the history of the American novel, but it is long out of print, and a plot summary is necessary here.

The novel concerns the adventures in Mexico of the hero from about 1820 to the end of 1822. Francis Berrian, graduating from Harvard, resolves to go West to seek his fortune. He travels down the Ohio and the Mississippi and then up the Red River to Alexandria, where he joins a group of men heading northwest in order to buy horses and mules from the Indians. They go up the Arkansas River to the foot of Mount Pike (Pike's Peak). Berrian then crosses the mountains to visit a Comanche village in the valley of the Rio Grande. There he discovers a Spanish damsel in captivity, Doña Martha d'Alvaro. He maneuvers her escape and takes her to Santa Fe to her father, the Conde Alvaro, governor of the Mexican state of Durango. Of course Berrian falls in love, but Martha is already betrothed to one Don Pedro Guttierez, and Berrian suffers under the double stigma of being both Protestant and American. All he can do is worship Martha from afar and travel with the family to the Conde's castle in Durango. There, Berrian becomes English teacher to Martha, Don Pedro, and others. The Conde, unable to convert Berrian or to prevent his daughter from falling in love with him, orders Berrian to leave. Berrian joins a group of rebels, participates in a battle north of Durango, and Book I ends with the group preparing to assault San Antonio. In Book II, the Conde and his family arrive inopportunely at San Antonio; when the rebels take the city they are jailed.

Berrian, for love of Martha, assists them in their escape to
Chihuahua. Berrian returns to San Antonio in time for the
Battle of Palos Blancos, in which the royalists retake the city.
He is thrown into prison and barely saved from execution. On
the road to Durango for a trial, Berrian is rescued by the
Conde, who is now on the patriots' side. Berrian then spends
several months hiding out in the mountains near Durango,
caring for a German family, a father and his three daughters
—much to the disgust of Martha. Released from his protec-
tive obligations, Berrian goes to the city of Mexico to join
the conqueror Iturbide, who soon becomes a tyrant. Martha
is there too, of course, and nearly in the clutches of Don Pedro, now risen to a high office in the government. Berrian
goes off once more to participate in the counterrevolution at
Veracruz. After heroisms there he arrives at Xalapa to rescue
Martha in the nick of time from Don Pedro and to marry her
himself. The Conde is reconciled to Berrian by the provision
that any daughters are to become Catholics. Berrian returns
for a visit to his Massachusetts home, certain to live happily
ever after.

This summary intricacy of plot can be broken down into
six subject areas: Berrian's background, the Comanche village, the Spanish aristocracy, the Texan expedition, the mountain interlude, and the Mexican Revolution. With that
arrangement in mind, let us examine Flint's progressive departure from reality.

Berrian's background is Flint's background without the
ministry. Berrian was born near Boston of a Puritan family.
He went to Harvard, but was subject to visionary musings
and a fondness for travel books. He resolved to go west "for
future Wealth, greatness, and happiness," [8] inspired by his
romantic readings as was Flint. Like Flint, he went down the
Ohio and the Mississippi. Like Flint, he heard the tales of
the keelboatmen, right down to the man who claimed to be

[8] Timothy Flint, *Francis Berrian, or The Mexican Patriot* (2 vols.;
Boston: Cummings, Hilliard, 1826), I, 20. Future quotations from
this text are not footnoted.

part horse and part alligator. Like Flint, he went to Alexandria and was horrified by the crudity of the civilization he found there: "this was the reality of that picture, which to my imagination had been so delightful." Like Flint, Berrian went fire-hunting. Like Flint, Berrian fell deathly ill, became delirious, recovered, and went to Natchitoches. And there, on page 39, the Berrian-Flint realism ends. As Berrian leaves for the Arkansas valley, Flint's writing decays. Compare quotations. The first describes the primitive life at the mouth of the Red River:

You rise from a sleep attained under such auspices, and crawl up the greasy banks to the cabins of the woodcutters. You see here inhabitants of an appearance and countenance in full keeping with the surrounding scenery. There is scarcely one of them but what has a monstrous protuberance in the stomach, sufficiently obvious to the eye, vulgarly called an "ague-cake," a yellowish white complexion, finely described in the language of the country, by the term "tallow face." There is an indercribable [*sic*] transparency of the skin, which seems to indicate water between the cuticle and the flesh. Eyes, preternaturally rolling and brilliant, glare in the centre of a large, morbid circle, in which the hues of red, black, and yellow are mixed. The small children bear all these dismal markings of the climate in miniature. Dirty and ragged, as mischievous as they are deformed, they roll about upon the slippery clay with an agility and alertness, from their appearance altogether incredible; for you would suppose them too feeble and clumsy to move. There is something unique, chilling, and cadaverous in the persons of both old and young. You would suppose that the grave was dug for them.

It is not fiction but fact, detailed, even moving. But fourteen pages later Flint writes like this:

The sun, which had burnished all the tops of the mountains with gold, and here and there glistened on banks of snow, would not shine into the valley, until he had almost gained his meridian height. The natives, fleet as the deer when on expeditions abroad, and at home lazy and yawning, were just issuing forth from their cabins, and stretching their limbs supinely in the cool of the morning. The smoke of their cabin fires had begun to undulate and whiten in horizontal pillars athwart the valley. The distant roar of the cascade, like the gong in Chinese music, seemed to mingle and harmonize all other sounds in the valley. It was a charming assemblage of strong contrasts, rocky and inaccessible mountains, the deep and incessant roar of the stream, a valley that seemed to sleep between these impregnable ramparts of nature . . . a spot sequestered like a lonely isle in the midst of the ocean; in the midst of it a busy, simple, and undescribed people, whose forefathers had been born and had died there for uncounted generations: a people, who could record wars, loves, and all the changes of fortune, if they had their historian. Such was the valley of the Comanches.

Berrian has moved from the foot of Mount Pike up the Arkansas River (which is not near Pike's Peak at all) and over to South Park, Colorado, where there are no pawpaws, persimmons, laurels, or nightingales, as Flint maintains. Even if one did not know this (and his contemporaries would not), surely one can sense the generalizing quality of the prose and its derivative nature: Berrian's Comanche village saw its first light in Chateaubriand's *Atala*. Berrian retires to a bower of weeping willows and magnolias, watches the parakeets flit by, and misquotes slightly lines of Pope's "Ode on Solitude":

> Here would I live, unnotic'd and unknown,
> Here unlamented would I die;
> Steal from the world, and not a stone
> Tell where I lie.

Next, Berrian meets two females, apt examples of the split between romanticism and realism in Flint's writing. The first is a six-foot-one-inch Indian named Red Heifer who is soon proposing marriage to Berrian. The second is Martha Migueles — "a vision, as fair as the poet's dream" — whose first words indicate her romantic function in the novel: "I am an unhappy captive. . . ."

There doesn't seem to be much point in tracking down Flint's sources. It is obvious that he took Berrian up to Colorado to take advantage of the recently published (1810) journal of Captain Zebulon Pike. Berrian's route south parallels Pike's exactly. Once he had Berrian in Mexico, Flint probably used the recently published work of William Bullock, *Six Months' Residence and Travels in Mexico* (London, 1824), the first work on Mexico published in English in the preceding hundred years. But it is now clear how little of his book has been taken directly from his friend Bullard. However, the sources do not matter, for Flint has given up any idea of relating the land to the people or of writing from the base of his own experience. At one stage he has Berrian apologize: "I might give you a sketch of the particulars of my journey from Durango to the city of Mexico, but it would betray me into details, beyond my purpose." What he means is that it would betray his own ineptitude. For Flint's real purpose is high romance, culled from European sources. The chapters are headed by quotations from Quevedo and Lope de Vega. The text makes references to Dante, Byron, Falstaff, Rousseau, Chateaubriand, Virgil, Mrs. Radcliffe, Wordsworth, Young, Sterne, Milton, Plato, Collins, Defoe, Ossian, Swedenborg, Cicero, Rochefoucauld, and Thomson — supported, ornamented, so to speak, by standard allusions; and as for the West, anything beyond the Sabine River, it is dreamlike, melancholy, literary, anything but real.

With some exasperation one looks beyond Doña Martha for some realistic character. There are good Indians and bad Indians, good Spanish and bad, a German servant, a loyal Irish servant Bryan O'Flaherty, complete with dialect, but only one believable character, the Rev. Thomas S——, who appears but briefly. The history of the West is subsidiary to the romance of lifeless characters.

It is easy now to see what Flint has done. Disillusioned about his own experiences, disillusioned by his own lack of success as a minister and by his own physical failings, he has created a fantasy for himself. Berrian is an idealized Flint who went west to make his fortune, and succeeded where Flint had failed. After the purging sickness, Berrian's good health returns and a great physical attractiveness is revealed: Berrian is loved by Red Heifer, Martha, three German girls, and a friend of Martha in Mexico City. Berrian's vigor extends to great courage in battle, acknowledgment as a national hero, and a triumphant return to his New England home to the envy of all, instead of Flint's craven crawling home to die. Berrian is recognizably Flint, waving an American flag in one hand and carrying a Protestant Bible in the other, but he has none of Flint's failings or disappointments. Flint's Berrian is Flint reborn into Eden. The Western setting is simply a setting, as incidental and ill-observed as that of Chateaubriand, and so of course the novel is not about the West at all.

The writing of the *Recollections* and *Francis Berrian* transformed Flint from a disappointed minister into a novelist, historian, biographer, and editor, culminating in his infamous production, the *Biographical Memoir of Daniel Boone* (1833). Flint had something more to say about the West, however, which concerns us here. His travels brought him in 1827 to Cincinnati and to the inspired idea of a journal for Western writings. Ignorant of the fact that a previous literary journal had existed there and failed, Flint began his *Western Monthly Review* in May, 1827. It lasted for three years, accumulated $3,000 in unpaid subscriptions, and collapsed in May, 1830. But it was a unique publication, fostering literature in the "West."

Flint's timing in 1827 had something to do with the spurning by Boston journals (*The United States Literary Gazette* and the *North American Review*) of a manuscript of his, a series of letters by "Martha Miguela Berrian," chatty affairs on the contrasts of manners and mores of the Americas. There is some personal spite, then, in the "Editor's Address" in the first issue: "We have seen, and we therefore know what one, who has not seen can not know, with what a curl of the lip, and crook of the nose an Atlantic reviewer contemplates the idea of a work written west of the Alleghany mountains. What, say they, a back woods man write! A poet make verses on Red river near the borders of Arkansas! Who ever heard of any thing worth remembering, that was written any where, except in Europe, or at least in Boston, or New York?"[9] The sample of Martha Berrian's letters included in the first issue would hardly impress an unprejudiced critic, but literary sectionalism has reared its ugly head. Flint furthered the split in his article on the "National Character of the Western People" (July, 1827) and in his long list of "Writers of the Western Country" (June, 1828). Western literature had, he said, "a vigor, an energy, a recklessness of manner and form, but a racy freshness of matter, which smacks strongly of our peculiar character and position. . . . Yet they of the Atlantic country, when they speak of us, curl the scornful lip, as though we were backwood's ignoramusses."[10] Such sectional defensiveness would become typical of the West, and make even more difficult the passage of writing from West to East.

Yet the embarrassing truth is that the *Western Monthly Review* was far more Eastern than Western, that "West" for Flint meant in theory the Mississippi valley but in practice the Ohio valley, and that there weren't any significant "Western" writers at all: Flint wrote his three volumes of the *Review* almost singlehandedly. Further, aside from excerpts from Flint's novels and the abominable poetry of his son Micah, the *Review* had little fiction, and only the dullest of nonfiction, condensed from Flint's catholic reading of everything from Shakespeare to Napoleon. Flint's prose in the *Review* is, at its best, uninspired. He used his journal to advertise his own work. The only "Western" work he published was an occasional story by James Hall, then in Vandalia, Illinois, a long way still from the West.

Hall's work had certain qualities which were later to be identified as Western and it certainly fit the characteristics Flint spelled out above. So we turn to Hall, who was to pick

[9] Timothy Flint, "Editor's Address," *Western Monthly Review,* I (May, 1827), 10.

[10] Timothy Flint, "Writers of the Western Country," *Western Monthly Review,* II (June, 1828), 21.

up the idea of a Western journal when Flint left off and continue that vain plea for a literature of the West for another
six years.

James Hall (1793-1868) had literary advantages, if you can
call them that, which Flint never had. His mother and his
three brothers were all writers, intimately involved with the
Port Folio. James was raised with literature, but he balanced
his book education with experiences in the War of 1812.
When he left the army in 1818, he studied law for two years
and then went west in search of adventure, following Flint
down the Ohio. He settled in Shawneetown, Illinois, for six
years; there he practiced law, became a prosecuting attorney
for ten counties, and then a circuit judge. He dabbled with
part-ownership in a local newspaper (*Illinois Gazette*), then
eased into politics and became state treasurer of Illinois. He
moved to Vandalia, the capital of Illinois, bought a share in
another newspaper (*Illinois Intelligencer*), and indulged in
literature as a pastime. His *Letters from the West*, primarily
on his trip westward down the Ohio, was published in London in 1828.

In the same year Hall edited *The Western Souvenir, a
Christmas and New Year's Gift for 1829*, a miscellany noted
primarily for the tale of Mike Fink by Morgan Neville. The
adopted sectionalism and the crusading aim are made clear
in Hall's preface: "It is written and published in the Western
country, by Western men, and is chiefly confined to subjects
connected with the history and character of the country which
gives it birth."[11] Though subsequent annuals were announced, none followed; indeed, Hall himself had to supply
about half the material in this first venture.

Undaunted, Hall attempted a monthly journal, the *Illinois*

[11] Quoted by John T. Flanagan, *James Hall, Literary Pioneer of
the Ohio Valley* (Minneapolis: University of Minnesota Press, 1941),
p. 53. Biographical details are from this book and from Randolph C.
Randall, *James Hall, Spokesman of the New West* (Columbus: Ohio
State University Press, 1964).

Monthly Magazine (October, 1830–September, 1832). Once more the Western optimism: "Every topic connected with the arts, the industry, or the resources of this flourishing state, or of the western country, will come within the scope of this work, and will receive from us such attention as our abilities will admit, or our opportunities for collecting information will allow." [12] Once more Hall himself wrote most of the material — two-thirds of each of the three volumes — and he did not make enough money to pay his expenses.

Politically estranged in Illinois, Hall moved in 1832 to Cincinnati, the "Athens of Western America," [13] and tried again. The *Western Monthly Magazine* (January, 1833–June, 1836) subscription list soared to 3,000 subscribers (at $3.50 a year), and at the end of three years the unpaid subscriptions totaled $7,000-$10,000.[14] Still, Hall did not have to write as much as previously. He announced that thirty-seven people had contributed to the second volume, most of these from the Ohio valley, but one from the "West" (Mrs. Ann Peyre Dinnies of St. Louis, who wrote the insipid poetry signed "Moira"). Hall's journal ended in the loss of subscribers, paid and unpaid, when he defended Catholicism. A succeeding journal edited by others, the *Western Monthly Magazine, and Literary Journal*, lasted one more year, to June, 1837.

Flint and Hall were too early with their periodicals. But it can be safely said that from 1827 to 1837, any "Western" writer of any quality at all had available to him a medium for publication. However, the only "Western" writers of any worth were the editors themselves. Beyond that, Flint and Hall, even though they did not necessarily do as they said, delineated the special qualities of "Western" writing. Specifically, they championed a unique language, energy, and an individualism peculiar to the wilderness — and these qualities are most evident in the work of Hall.

Hall painted genre pictures of the frontier (predating, in-

[12] Quoted by Flanagan, p. 57.
[13] James Hall, quoted in *ibid.*, p. 63.
[14] *Ibid.*, p. 75.

cidentally, those of Simms and Kennedy), calling particular attention to language, italicizing every colloquialism. He described one character, for example, as follows: "All the time he was ranting and roaring in praise of himself, his horse, and the United States of America. He boasted that he was born in the woods, rocked in a sugar trough, and suckled by a buffalo; that he could tote a steamboat, and outrun a streak of lightning; that his wife was as handsome as a pet fawn, and his children *real roarers*."[15] He could write with humor:

"I don't know what cold is good for, except to give a man an appetite for his luqor——"
"Or long nights," continued the host, "but to get sober in——"[16]

He created at least two distinctive characters. In *Harpe's Head* there is the snake-killer Hank Short, the dwarfish adolescent raised in the swamps of North Carolina, addicted to killing a snake by taking it by the back in his teeth and shaking it. Another is the murderer Micajeh Harpe, whose severed head gives the book its title.

Finally, Hall had much to say on the relationship of man to his environment. An extended passage will give some of the flavor of his writing (so much better than Flint's) as well as make the point:

It is true, that our people had some vague notions of their own importance, and would sometimes talk of their *birth-rights* and their *future greatness* in a strain that would make a stranger stare. Accustomed to the contemplation of great mountains, long rivers, and boundless plains, the majestic features of their country swelled their ideas, and gave a ting of romance to their conceptions. The immense cotton-woods and sycamores that overhung their rivers, the huge alligator that bellowed in the stream, and the great mammoth bones imbedded in their swamps became familiar standards of comparison; while their long journeys over boundless plains teeming with the products of nature, gave them exalted notions of

[15] James Hall, *The Soldier's Bride and Other Tales* (Philadelphia: Key and Biddle, 1833), p. 107.
[16] James Hall, *Legends of the West* (Cincinnati: Applegate, 1857), p. 126.

the magnificence of their country. One would have thought they were speaking in parables, who heard them describing the old thirteen states as a mere appendage of the future republic—a speck on the map of the United States—a sort of out-lot with a cotton field at one end and a manufactory of wooden clocks at the other; yet they were in sober earnest.[17]

 It is clear that if Western literature were ever to come into its own, taking the advice of the sectionalists Flint and Hall, that literature would be different in form and content from Eastern literature. As long as Eastern romantic standards prevailed, there would be in the West a kind of bastard literature, a grafting of the scenic effects of the West to the sentimentality of the East, and a resultant absurd distortion. It is as if a true Western literature had to wait for someone to be born in the West who would know no other standards. Hall once described Flint as "the very Daniel Boon [*sic*] of bookmakers."[18] That was in 1833, two years before Samuel Clemens was born. Meanwhile, Washington Irving was to go west —and ignore completely the sound advice of Flint and Hall.

[17] *Ibid.*, pp. 369–370.
[18] James Hall, review of Flint's *Lectures, Western Monthly Magazine*, I (June, 1833), 264.

4

THE EASTERNERS:
Washington Irving and
Francis Parkman

The expatriate Washington Irving in 1832, at the age of forty-nine, can be described as at his wits' end. He had nearly exhausted his Spanish materials, the result of a scholarly but dilatory four years in Spain. Rescued from Spain by friends and named secretary to the American legation at London, he had sunk there into a social lethargy for two more years, until a change of administration in the summer of 1831 ended his appointment. He might have been content to go on indefinitely repeating his stock of Spanish stories, but his English publisher bypassed his agent in order to write Irving directly and tell him precisely how much money he, Murray, had lost on the last two books — *Columbus* (1828) and *Granada* (1829) — and then cut in half the fee for Irving's new book, *Voyages and Discoveries of the Companions of Colum-*

bus (1831).[1] Irving had had enough. He switched publishers and headed home, nervously.

He was uneasy about his reception in America, but he need not have been. A gala dinner in New York on May 30, 1832, assured him of America's respect, and his book *The Alhambra*, published a week later, received splendid reviews. But there is no hiding his restlessness and aimlessness as he spent the summer in frantic touring — to Philadelphia, Baltimore, Washington, to West Point and the Catskills, to Boston and the White Mountains, to Saratoga Springs, and then onto a Lake Erie steamboat headed for Detroit with a pair of travelers he had met that spring at Le Havre. His mood must have been one of what-shall-I-do-next? for it took little persuasion to get him to change his plans and head out for the wild West. He needed new materials for a fresh start; here was the opportunity. And why not?

He would be the first professional American writer to go west of St. Louis, the first skilled author to write about the West on the basis of firsthand experience. I discount here without discussion Cooper's *The Prairie* (1828), written out of whole cloth by a man who had never been west of the Finger Lakes. The West — any foreign country — deserved a more significant, more accurate treatment than that. Fiction too far removed from fact is as lopsided as a history book without an adjective. Cooper's West is as second-rate as the thousands of Westerns modeled on it. Irving's West is — unfortunately — more East than West.

But Irving had been presented with a unique opportunity. His invitation to the West had been extended by one Henry Leavitt Ellsworth, newly appointed as one of three Indian commissioners sent to establish order and justice in the area of the Arkansas River where Creek, Choctaw, Cherokee, and Delaware Indians lived uneasily with white squatters and

[1] All biographical details are taken from Stanley T. Williams, *The Life of Washington Irving* (2 vols.; New York: Oxford, 1935), II, 1–91, and from Pierre M. Irving, *The Life and Letters of Washington Irving* (4 vols.; New York: Putnam, 1869), II, 207–336.

marauding Osages and Pawnees.[2] Ellsworth, on his way to
Fort Gibson, Arkansas, invited Irving to come along, and
with Irving his two traveling companions, the Englishman
Charles Joseph Latrobe and the young Swiss Count Albert-
Alexandre de Pourtalès. It is difficult to justify the latter in-
vitation.

Still, Irving must have found them congenial and interesting. Latrobe he described as a citizen of the world, a botanist,
a geologist, a butterfly collector, and a sportsman — indefatig-
able, busy, always cheerful.[3] Latrobe had been an avid mountain climber in Switzerland and there met Pourtalès. The relationship is not clear, but Latrobe seems to have been tutor
to the nineteen-year-old count, under contract to educate him
or at least to keep him out of Switzerland until he reached
his majority — "to sow his wild oats in a foreign country," as
Ellsworth put it. Pourtalès was avid to do just that; specifically, to find an Indian mistress among the Osages. Lively,
wild, impetuous, joyful, galliard, frivolous, sensuous, romantic — all these terms were used by Ellsworth and Irving to
describe him.

These gentlemen, then — the stuff of fiction — left Cincinnati September 3, 1832, on the steamboat *Messenger* bound
for St. Louis. What would we give for a complete description of that trip through the various stages of the frontier:
the boat ride down the Ohio and up to St. Louis; the visit on
September 13 with Governor William Clark; the visit on September 14 to Fort Jefferson to see the recently captured Black
Hawk; the ride across Missouri to Independence and then

[2] Stanley T. Williams and Barbara D. Simpson, eds., *Washington
Irving on the Prairie or A Narrative of a Tour of the Southwest in
the Year 1832 by Henry Leavitt Ellsworth* (New York: American
Book, 1937), pp. x-xi. Future quotations from this text are not footnoted.

[3] Washington Irving, *A Tour on the Prairies*, edited with an intro-
ductory essay by John Francis McDermott (copyright 1956 by the University of Oklahoma Press, Norman), p. 12. Future quotations from this
text are not footnoted.

south, with nightly stops at missions, to Fort Gibson, arriving there October 8. The fort was garrisoned by a detachment of Rangers, mounted men who had enlisted for short terms of service, but most of these had just been sent off southwest on an exploring expedition. Ellsworth found no other commissioners at the fort, nor secretary either; so he named Irving secretary pro tem at $5 a day and promptly set out in pursuit of the Rangers. Pourtalès dragged Latrobe off in another direction in hot pursuit of an Osage party, but rejoined Ellsworth and Irving just when the latter two were congratulating themselves on being rid of the count. All soon joined the Rangers for a month of riding on a circle route in the prairies of eastern present-day Oklahoma.

Such is the basis for Irving's *A Tour on the Prairies* (1835). Actually, it was not a very significant tour. There was no military action, except for one brief alert, and nothing much to explore in that barren area. The time was spent in hunting —wild horses, buffalo, deer, and Pourtalès, who managed to get lost one night. The party returned to Fort Gibson on November 8, and Irving went rapidly back east via New Orleans.

The only really memorable point in this affair is the presence of Irving. Through him this tour of the prairie became something more than a minor episode in American history. For Irving kept a journal in which to record his experiences. Each day he went through a ritual of writing, first washing himself and tidying up the things in his tent in order to make his ideas "flow properly," and then recording events, the occurrences worthy of remembrance, the foundations on which he would later build his fabric. This journal, first published in 1919, is remarkable. For example: "Picturesque scene of the camp — some roasting bear's meat and venison — others stretching & dressing skins — some lying on skins in the shade — horses feeding — hunters coming in with game — turkeys, &c. — groups relating the morning's exploits — clothes hang-

ing to dry — tent pitched — fine luncheon." [4] These disjointed
phrases sketch in a complete picture, down to the fine detail
of "clothes hanging to dry," and we are reminded that Irving's *Sketch Book* was written by Geoffrey Crayon, Esq., the
"Geoffrey" recalling the story-telling of Chaucer, the "Crayon" the on-the-spot sketching, and the "Esquire" defining a
point of view. Beyond this, Irving *colored* his sketches:
"Creeks — calico hunting shirts — scarlet & blue hankerchief
round head — leather & scarlet leggings. . . ." He also
animated them, going beyond the power of mere still
lifes: "at daybreak imitations of cocks crowing, hens cack-
ling, among the youngsters of the camp — horses driven in
— breakfast — whistling — singing — dancing — hallooing after horses — joking, laughing, scampering after horses . . ."
so that there is a sense of perpetual life. And occasionally
Irving tried for the actual sounds of voices: "My gun is so
powerful dirty"; "My horse goes quite peart." He made notes
on individuals so that he could later build character: "Antoine thorough Frenchman — vaunts, exults, sings, boasts." He
reminded himself of anecdotes which he could expand later:
"Story of Uncle Sam's gun." And he remembered this: "Mr.
Portales boots lost on the road — one was found — a Creek Indian was seen with the lost boot on, looking for the other."
Consider, too, the poetry inherent in such an entry as this:
"Make my bed under a big tree on a hillock among long, dry,
Prarie grass —a superb couch — sleep soundly sweetly warm-
ly tho a heavy dew fell — Starlight — watch the stars on the
prairie as at sea."

I submit that there is a genius to this last passage, however
rough and unshaped it is. Compare it with the work of another writer in the following parallel passage:

I delighted to wake in the stillness of the long night, and to rouse
my spirit from its lethargy; to open my eyes upon the deep blue

[4] Washington Irving, *The Western Journals of Washington Irving*,
edited and annotated by John Francis McDermott (copyright 1944 by
the University of Oklahoma Press, Norman), p. 133. Future quotations
from this text are not footnoted.

sky, with its host of stars, overhead; to glance upon the dying fires and sleeping camp; to muse upon the past and the present; to raise my heart to heaven; — and, without taking care for the future, to bless God for a portion of those sweet and healthful thoughts which spring from a calm and contented spirit, and incite my soul to gratitude for this lull and calm in the midst of the heaving and restless sea of existence.[5]

This is vague, misty writing, clouded with sentiment; it could have been written anywhere. Actually, it was written by Latrobe, same time, same place. Latrobe too kept a journal and later published a version of it as chapters in *The Rambler in North America* (1835). His book covered various American travels, but most of it is in the same generalizing, poetical, rambling tone which lacks immediacy or a sense of reality. Consider another Latrobe passage: "The whole scene was highly picturesque as you looked upon the river, gliding at the base of a range of high rocky hills, with the thick forests arrayed in the glorious hues of autumn, and saw the bright flame-coloured sands sprinkled by groups of horsemen and piles of luggage." It lacks the fine specific detail of Irving's journal, and unfortunately it says nothing. Latrobe couldn't write, and yet he knew better. His book is presented in the form of letters to a younger brother, and the first letter recalls the pithy advice of a friend: "let your letters, in short, be about men, and not about mountains, and let them inform me what I have never heard, not what has been presented to the world a hundred times before." Precisely. This advice helps us realize the comparative brilliance of Irving's receptive eye and ear.

And still another journal was kept on the Oklahoma tour, this one by Ellsworth, which comes to us in the form of a lengthy letter to his wife, not published until 1937, a retrospective confidential summary of the trip as told by a matter-of-fact Connecticut Yankee. Ellsworth is chatty, informa-

---

[5] Charles Joseph Latrobe, *The Rambler in North America* (3 vols.; London: R. S. Seeley and W. Burnside, 1835), I, 199. Future quotations from this text are not footnoted.

tive, simple, straightforward — and obnoxiously moral. For
example: "Mʳ Pourteles & Brailey have nothing but moccas-
sins and their feet are wet every moment — How foolish it is
for common citizens to take such an excursion, without shoes
or boots? — It is more Indian; and there seems to be a disposition among most white men, who come to this country
to step into indian habits & customs — for my part I wish
to keep as seperate as possible from them." Sometimes
he does better: "The night was cold — we made a large fire
and laying blanketts down around it, so that our feet would
be warm we went to bed, and slept tolerably well — having
covered up our heads as little children do to keep off witches
— The distance travelled today was 28 miles on a true course
with the exception of a bend, made after our stop at noon to
avoid a deep ravine. . . ." Ellsworth has no sense of proportion, no sense of what is significant, and little ability to put
events into words. Sometimes, though, he is better than Irving.
Two parties of hunters saw each other at such a distance
that they came tearing back to camp alerting the Rangers to a
party of five hundred armed Pawnees just ahead. Ellsworth is
delightful:

What *consternation*! I cannot describe it. . . . Oh! the confusion!
the cooking dishes were upset as matters of no moment, for many
a poor soul, thought he should need no more nourishment — Some
actually shed *tears* — Mʳ Irving could find only one *Leggin*, and
he was calling through the camp loud, and louder still, for his odd
leggin, of mighty little consequence in a battle — He was as *pale*
as he could be, and much terrified — Latrobe seized his saddle,
and put it on wrong side before and girted it in this manner —
Pourteles wanted to know, whether it was best to take saddle bags
or not? One young chap went running around, wringing his hands,
crying, "Lord jesus help me find my bridle"!

Yet he ends the passage with his usual morality:

Yes I never shall forget the feelings I had — I thought of *home* —
of *you* & the dear children and committing myself to God, I felt
resigned and do believe I should have fought bravely untill
death —

Ellsworth was suitably perceptive, but he lacked the urge or the power to turn his journal into literature.

So did Irving.

The sad truth is that Irving's *A Tour on the Prairies* is but a pale reflection of his vivacious journals, and an attempt should be made to spell out why.

Irving left Fort Gibson in November, 1832. He spent the winter in Washington, fascinated by the session of Congress. In April, 1833, he took a nephew on a tour of Virginia. In August he was back for the season at Saratoga Springs. In October he returned to Washington and then went on another tour of the Catskills, this time with Martin Van Buren. In November he was busy writing again— what we don't know — living in New York with his brother Ebenezer. A year later, November, 1834, he had finished the *Tour*, which was finally published in April, 1835, as Volume I of *The Crayon Miscellany* — three volumes of warmed-over manuscripts were published that year.

The delay in writing reflects the difficulty in making a work of art out of an experience. How should he shape the material? First of all, he chose a geographic unity, cutting out his experiences before reaching Fort Gibson and those after his departure — a sound literary procedure. Second, he chose a character to emphasize: not Ellsworth, not Latrobe, not Pourtalès, not himself, but a squire, groom, cook, or factotum, a French creole named Antoine Deshertes and nicknamed Tonish. Out of very few notes in the journal, Irving created a "Gil Blas of the frontiers," a comic servant given to telling audacious tales. It does not matter that Irving's Tonish had little resemblance to the original Antoine — who is reputed to have said concerning his portrait, "Let me meet Irving on one of the Prairies and one or other of us shall lose his scalp!" As John Francis McDermott has pointed out, Irving's created character is singularly flat — Irving complacently superior and relying on a stale literary tradition, rather than on his accu-

rate journal.[6] Tonish is a literary device, and one that failed in
its effect. Third, Irving shaped his material by not shaping it;
embarrassed for any actual plot, he must have pondered using some such fantasy as Cooper had written. Wisely, he
chose to be honest with his materials: "It is a simple narrative [he wrote apologetically in his introduction] of every
day occurrences; such as happen to every one who travels the
prairies. I have no wonders to describe, nor any moving accidents by flood or field to narrate." Nevertheless, as we have
seen in the *Journals,* Irving had the literary skill to make even
this simple narrative interesting. Why did he not?

Discretion (an Eastern invention) prevented him. With a
reputation at stake as being second only to Cooper as America's greatest writer, Irving had no choice but to tone down
the facts. He might relish Ellsworth's lecturing to Pourtalès
concerning the future "deep mortification" at the possibility
of the "apperance of red progeny, who will rise up and call
him father!" but he could not, of course, print this. He might
privately snort at the ridiculous ineptness of the amateur
Rangers; but he was too concerned for his reputation to insult democracy in so many words. If he saw the obscene Indian drawings which Ellsworth saw, he doesn't say so. He
was too genteel. Irving wrote on an Osage village: "Here the
Commissioner made a speech from on horseback; informing
his hearers of the purport of his mission. . . . This speech
. . . seemed to have a pacifying effect upon the multitude."
But Ellsworth had written privately: "and when I was ad-
dressing them and urging them to peace . . . these little boys
made water before all the women, and even *upon* some of
them, laughing." The raw history was too much for Irving
— or for any writer for decades to come.

Romanticism (another Eastern invention) limited him. The
absence of castles in America — one outcropping of rock Ellsworth derisively dubbed "Irvings castle" — or, in other words,
the absence of a historical past continued to embarrass American writers of this period. Irving tried to make up for this in

[6] Washington Irving, *A Tour,* pp. 50–54.

his published *Tour* by inserting references to Europe. Tele-machus, Nestor, Gil Blas, Adonis, Napoleon, the hero of La Mancha, Lycurgus, Draco, Robin Hood, Claude Lorraine, Scaramouch, Pantaloon, nomads, gypsies, knights-errant, ban-ditti, and Moorish castles — these are the bases of comparison with which Irving tried to reach his readers. They betray his own bias, his inability to see in the West anything as existent by itself, without a romantic glow. "Picturesque" — the word recurs time and again as Irving sketches a scene and is satis-fied with it when it is only "picturesque."

But the worst limitation is the language. It is strange that he even bothers with the vernacular in his *Journals* because the *Tour* either omits it or dresses it up. Conversations be-come leaden:

"That must be a prairie set on fire by the Osage hunters," said the Captain.

"It is at Red Fork," said Beatte, regarding the sky. "It seems but three miles distant, yet it perhaps is twenty."

The fine scene of the Pawnee scare given previously by Ells-worth becomes in Irving's polished prose absurd:

"Where is my saddle?" cried one. "Has any one seen my rifle?" cried another. "Who will lend me a ball?" cried a third, who was loading his piece. "I have lost my bullet-pouch." "For God's sake help me to girth this horse!" cried another; "he's so restive I can do nothing with him."

Irving is palliative. Observe the softening process in Irving's polishing-up of a journal item. The journal had said:

Bugle sounds at daybreak — bustle in camp — catching horses — driving them in — Have you seen my horse? cries one. What horse is that broke loose over the brook? Night guard comes in — dis-missed — fires made — breakfast preparing — some packing — blan-kets that have formed tents dismantled — singing — laughing — joking, whooping — saddling horses.

When he wrote the *Tour*, the passage had become:

At the signal-note of the bugle, the sentinels and patrols marched in from their stations around the camp and were dismissed. The rangers were roused from their night's repose, and soon a bustling

scene took place. While some cut wood, made fires, and prepared
the morning's meal, others struck their foul-weather shelter of
blankets, and made every preparation for departure; while others
dashed about, through bush and brake, catching the horses and
leading or driving them into camp.

During all this bustle the forest rang with whoops, and shouts,
and peals of laughter.

He could not, it seems, write without clichés: "made every
preparation for departure," "through bush and brake," "the
forest rang," and "peals of laughter." The rewrite is remarkably dull.

He had the ability and he had the opportunity to do better
work. Why did he do less? I think because in his literary in-
security he tried to please — and tried only that.

This brief study of the *Tour* helps explain Irving's gross
distortions in two more fictionalized versions of American history. The *Tour* sold very well, at home and abroad, enabling
Irving to buy his future home, Sunnyside. Even before the
Tour was printed, Irving had put a nephew to work sorting
out John Jacob Astor's papers, and in 1836 he himself moved
into Astor's home to add to Pierre Irving's injudicious borrowings his own *"filligree work"* — "extending some facts,
touching up others, enriching and embellishing."[7] His own
words thus describe the failings of *Astoria* (1836). That book
paid well too, enabling Irving to finance extensive additions
to Sunnyside and the purchase of eight more acres of land
as well. No sooner had he finished with Astor than he bought
a journal from Captain Benjamin Bonneville and translated
that into his own peculiar tongue. *Bonneville* (1837) was
written at Sunnyside — from that point of view, so to speak.
It sold well too. One month in the wild West paid Irving
handsome dividends indeed.

Irving had used history to write a form of fiction — fiction
because it certainly was not history. He applied a nineteenth-
century romantic gloss to his Western subjects — he had to,
both because of his own penchant and because of the tastes

[7] Washington Irving quoted in *Life and Letters*, II, 302.

of his readers — a gloss which did not enhance but which obscured and befogged the historical reality. Between that saint Leatherstocking and that imp Tonish, Cooper and Irving had set limits to the future fiction on the West. Irving's *Tour*, therefore, represents a sort of first and last chance to do poetic justice to reality in the West. As history or as fiction, it failed to have a lasting significance. Irving, the only skilled eyewitness, had found no way to transform that perishable reality into a lasting truth.

What we are searching for, I suppose, is someone intelligent and literate enough to sense and to record with some degree of honesty the rapidly changing history of a nascent land. To record and to shape — but to shape without the restrictions of the genteel tradition of the past. A younger man could, perhaps, avoid the harnesses of an Irving, and Francis Parkman is the next most likely candidate as the writer of the West. Young, intelligent, sensitive, acute, literate, and on the spot — Parkman was all these things; but, like Irving, he was born to traditions of the East which were to make his work on the West something less than perfect.

Parkman's most recent biographers, Mason Wade and Howard Doughty, have both written of the transformation which occurred between the writing of the Western journal in 1846, the publication of a first version of the journal in the *Knickerbocker Magazine*, 1847–49, and its final version as *The Oregon Trail*, 1849. (The actual title in 1849 was *The California and Oregon Trail; Being Sketches of Prairie and Rocky Mountain Life*. The present title was given to the fourth edition, 1872.) We need do little more here than summarize their biographies and then choose between their interpretations. Wade finds the book "diluted triply by the circumstances of its composition."[8] Doughty is not so sure that "Brahmin

[8] Mason Wade, ed., *The Journals of Francis Parkman* (2 vols.; New York: Harper, 1947), II, 385. Further quotations from this text are not footnoted. See also Mason Wade, *Francis Parkman, Heroic Historian* (New York: Viking, 1942), pp. 286–302.

snobberies" circumscribed Parkman's view of the West.[9] The base from which Parkman wrote must be spelled out.

We must think in terms of a man only twenty-two years old when he went west, a Bostonian, independently rich and unattached, not even to his Federalist, mercantilist, Unitarian background, but attached since his sophomore year at Harvard (and his initial exposure to Jared Sparks) to the life of a historian. Along with this scholarly urge was an overriding physical urge to excel, whether at rifle practice, boxing lessons, hiking and climbing, or horseback riding, an urge pushing him too frequently to the point of exhaustion. Whether one calls the breakdowns heart strains, as did Parkman, or hypertension, as does Doughty, either way the physical striving had great consequences for the writing of the historian.

He had early developed the habit of keeping journals of his travels, using them as a source book for his future histories and as a base for literary experiments. The first of these, a record of a summer excursion on the Magalloway River, Parkman had tried to shape into a narrative; but if we consider Parkman's youthful love of the works of Scott, Cooper, Byron, Coleridge, Milton, and Shakespeare, we are not surprised by Doughty's judgment that the narrative was "too often over-labored and 'literary' as compared with the direct, incisive prose of the journal."[10] Other journals followed, of trips into the wilderness of New England and Canada, of the trip to Europe in 1843–44, and these were translated into five sketches for the *Knickerbocker Magazine* of 1845 — essays, poetry, and fiction — which Doughty finds consciously literary: "The incidents from the journals, moreover, rather lose their original sharpness of touch as Parkman reshapes them to the conventions of fiction and recasts them in a more formal literary English."[11] And yet Parkman was clearly striving to

[9] Howard Doughty, *Francis Parkman* (New York: Macmillan, 1962), p. 117 ff.

[10] *Ibid.*, pp. 48–49.

[11] *Ibid.*, p. 95.

go beyond his literary environment. One of the sketches contains these lines:

Reader, these scenes are rude and savage, repulsive, no doubt, to the taste of literary epicures, and no less so to the transcendental "spiritualists" who infest this city of Boston. Highly flattered should I be if my humble narrative should be honored with their condemnation; and yet, to win the smiles of a larger and fairer portion of the readers of OLD KNICK, I would gladly make this history more smooth and attractive. But the rough and bold features of the original will lose all resemblance if I try to soften them upon the canvass; and an inexperienced and unskilful painter is doubly bound, in interest as well as conscience, to be faithful.[12]

If we translate this as a taste for wildness (an escapist urge), couple it with his youth (then twenty-one), and add Parkman's nervous energy, there is still a chance that the romantic schooling of his past will give way before this desire to write of things as they are.

But Parkman went west with only this much literary background, and he left off his historical research on the life of Pontiac only because another breakdown was imminent. Rather in a state of impatience, of desuetude, did Parkman agree to join his cousin Quincy Shaw on a hunting expedition on the Oregon Trail. Dutifully, he kept a journal of his trip.

Parkman was not about to become a democrat by the mere act of traveling west. He had not reached Fort Pitt before he noted in his journal a stage driver as "bluff, blisterous, profane, and coarse," and the stage passengers as "brutish clods." "Take an ordinary man of high education," he lectured himself, "and what sympathies can he have with such?" Obviously, he carried Harvard College and Boston with him and *observed* from the vantage point of a gentleman. Perhaps we will have to accept such a point of view to get anything written about the West at all. Parkman records of the boat landing at Independence in May, 1846, "The Baltimoreans got

[12] Francis Parkman, "A Fragment of Family History," *Knickerbocker Magazine*, XXV (June, 1845), 510. Quoted in part by Doughty, p. 98.

shamefully drunk, and one of them, an exquisite in full dress, tumbled into the Water." We have to be satisfied to have the incident recorded, however superior the author, and complain only that the detail is gracefully omitted from *The Oregon Trail.*

Parkman and Shaw were two young rich sportsmen out to see the sights and only vaguely conscious that they moved in a superb and perishing moment of American history. They hired a remarkably fine guide (Henry Chatillon) and a French-Canadian muleteer (Deslauriers) and embarked on the prairies — "the great green ocean" — early in May, joining emigrant parties only for the safety of their numbers. And when the weather grew hot and the prairies interminably flat, Parkman dreamed of forest country and a mountain spring cooling two bottles of champagne.

The trip lasted some five months — along the Platte River to Fort Laramie, a month with the Indians in southeastern Wyoming, south to the Arkansas River in Colorado, and east in September across Kansas, back to Independence. The experience seems not to have changed Parkman, if we can judge from his journal entry of September 21: "Camped at Dragoon Creek, after travelling 21 miles. Met waggons. 'Whar are ye from? Californy?' 'No.' 'Santy Fee?' 'No, the Mountains.' 'What yer been doing thar? Tradin'?' 'No.' 'Trappin'?' 'No.' 'Huntin'?' 'No.' 'Emigratin'?' 'No.' 'What *have* ye been doing then, God damn ye?' (Very loud, as we were by this time almost out of hearing.)" These lines, too, were omitted from *The Oregon Trail.* And yet Parkman ends his journal with these haunting lines of Milton:

> The mind is its own place, and in itself
> Can make a heaven of hell, a hell of heaven.

Why, I wonder, did he not include the preceding line: "A mind not to be chang'd by place or time"?

Parkman's trip had not cured his bodily and mental ills; rather, it had aggravated them. A month after his return, he moved to New York to consult a Dr. S. R. Elliott who owned a kind of sanitarium on Staten Island; by January, 1847, he had to submit to a "rest cure." His physical ailments were partial blindness, indigestion, and arthritis; these were accompanied (logically enough) by insomnia and hypochondria, themselves but symptoms of underlying stresses which have never been diagnosed. Nevertheless, the first chapter of the magazine version of *The Oregon Trail* appeared in the *Knickerbocker Magazine* only four months after his return. This version was written with the help of Quincy or Sarah Shaw or other volunteers who read aloud Parkman's journal to him and then took down the sentences he dictated. The last installment was timed to come out in the *Knickerbocker* after book publication in 1849 (to forestall the possibility of pirated texts). His eyes still too weak to read book proof, in September, 1848, Parkman accepted the offer of his cousin Charles Eliot Norton to assist him. Thus the triple distillation, or dilution, as Wade calls it. The journal is Parkman's own; the magazine version is Shaw's; the book, Norton's. Transformation there was, but it was not necessarily a dilution, as will be evident if we consider in reverse order the writing of the book in its two stages, from journal to magazine version and from magazine version to book form.

The revision of the magazine text must have begun in the late fall of 1848, two years after Parkman's return from the West. Parkman had been living in New York City or on Staten Island in that period; he had finished the magazine version of his book by September, 1847. In the spring of 1848 he had begun writing *Pontiac*; in the fall he had made a trip to a spa at Brattleboro, Vermont, where he had met his future wife; it was in September, 1848, that he accepted the help of Norton, who at that time was working for East India merchants in Boston, and Parkman moved back to Boston sometime that fall. Norton recalled late in his life the process of revision: "During my years in the counting-house a casual acquaintance with Frank Parkman developed into a friendship which lasted through life. He was then printing in the 'Knick-

erbocker Magazine,' if I remember rightly, his first book, 'The
Oregon Trail' and when it was to be published as a volume
he asked me to revise the numbers, and many an evening,
when there was not other work to be done, was spent by me
and him in the solitary counting-room in going over his
work." [13] His comment is not very detailed, but it must be
fitted to Parkman's letter accepting Norton's assistance, which
would appear to be critical of Norton's style; Parkman wrote,
referring to Norton's own writing: "Put a little pepper and
allspice into it — it will not harm its respectability." [14] Norton
would seem to be the more conservative stylist, but I do not
think he was much of a censor. The revisions of the two men
were such as to make the book better than the *Knickerbocker*
version. But there was to be another revision before the book
appeared in its present text, done when Parkman was forty-
eight. The preface to the fourth edition is dated "Boston,
March 30, 1872" and is preceded by the following note: "As
the early editions were printed in my absence, I did not correct the proofs, — a process doubly necessary, since the book
was written from dictation. The necessary corrections have
been made in the present edition." Doughty and Wade tell
us nothing of the circumstances of this revision. It will not
affect our purpose here to consider the two as one, but the
kinds of revisions must be detailed.

I would estimate that ninety-five out of each hundred
sentences were left unchanged. The changes made were like
the following:

Knickerbocker	*The Oregon Trail*
The rich and luxuriant woods	the woods
this strange migration	this migration
his obsequious politeness	his politeness
a cordial grunt of salutation	a grunt of salutation
a countenance of lofty indignation	a countenance of indignation

[13] Sarah Norton and M. A. DeWolfe Howe, eds., *Letters of Charles
Eliot Norton* (2 vols.; Boston: Houghton Mifflin, 1913), I, 27–28.
[14] Quoted by Wade, *Francis Parkman*, p. 302.

its virgin wildness	its wildness
Huge skulls	Skulls
hideous old hag	old hag
my hardy little mare Pauline	my horse
rude garments of skin	garments of skin
The large black carcasses	The carcasses
his handsome face	his face

Such a trimming of adjectival clichés might well have been applied to even more of the purple passages of *The Oregon Trail.* Nothing is lost when "the fine figure of the noble-hearted hunter, HENRY CHATILLON" becomes plain "Henry Chatillon."

Some few passages have been censored. "In the absence of liquor we offered him a cup of coffee" became "We offered him a cup of coffee." In *Knickerbocker,* Parkman recalls chasing a buffalo: "As my horse ran past him, within about twelve yards, I fired my remaining pistol, by a thoughtless impulse, striking him in the rump, too high for mortal effect"; the sentence was omitted in the book version. A passage on Parkman's medication — "Having within that time taken six grams of opium" — was omitted. His idle shooting at prairie dogs — "scooping out the brains of the unfortunate inhabitants with rifle bullets" — became in *The Oregon Trail* simply "shooting the unfortunate inhabitants." I do not find censorship of any more moment than this.

Long passages on two characters, "the Captain" and "Tête Rouge," have been omitted in the 1872 edition. I judge that in the interval of revision Parkman lost some of the irksomeness on which they were based. The characters were of peripheral interest, and nothing is missing when editing is done on a line like this: "As may well be conceived, these repeated instances of high-handed dealing sufficiently exasperated us."

Several passages in *Knickerbocker* contrast the East unfavorably with the West. Henry Chatillon is praised by comparison with "the polished fops of literature or fashion." An emigrant from Kentucky is described as a gentleman in comparison with "the vulgar and ignorant boors who float on the scum of fashion in some of our eastern cities." But the quality of *The Oregon Trail* is not much changed by the omission of such displays of temper.

A few moralizing paragraphs are omitted from the book, but with no loss to literature: "Truly it is a poor thing, this life of an Indian. . . . Yet never have I seen in any Indian village on the remote prairie such abject depravity, such utter abasement and prostitution of every nobler part of humanity, as I have seen in great cities, the centres of the world's wisdom and refinement." The narrative is tighter for the omissions.

We are left with one highly interesting group of passages in the *Knickerbocker* magazine which were excised before the fourth edition. In these Parkman contrasts the life in the West with his former life. In one long passage, he sits on a buffalo skull and contemplates the wild flowers with their haunting reminder of wild flowers in New England:

One travelling in this country seldom has leisure to think of any thing but the stern features of the scenery and its accompaniments, or the practical details of each day's journey. Like them, he and his thoughts grow hard and rough. . . . "There are good things," thought I, "in the savage life, but what can it offer to replace those powerful and ennobling influences that can reach unimpaired over more than three thousand miles of mountains, forests and deserts?"

Other examples follow:

And yet stern and wild associations gave a singular interest to the view; for here each man lives by the strength of his own arms and the valor of his own heart. Here the feeble succumb to the brave, with nothing to sustain them in their weakness. Here society is reduced to its original elements, the whole fabric of art and conventionality is struck rudely to pieces, and men find themselves suddenly brought back to the wants and resources of their original natures.

"The prairie is a strange place," said I. "A month ago I should have thought it a rather startling affair to have an acquaintance ride out in the morning and lose his scalp before night; but here it seems the most natural thing in the world."

I believe that few ever breathe that reckless atmosphere without becoming wholly indifferent to any evil chance that may befall themselves or their friends.

"Am I," I thought to myself, "the same man who, a few months since, was seated, a quiet student of belle-lettres, in a cushioned armchair by a sea-coal fire?"

To some of the spoiled children of cities it may seem strange, that men with no object in view should continue to follow a life of such hardship and desperate adventure, yet there is a mysterious, resistless charm in the basilisk eye of danger, fascinating that it may destroy, and few men perhaps remain long in that wild region without learning to love peril for its own sake, and to laugh carelessly in the face of death.

One other lesson our short prairie experience had taught us; that of profound contentment in the present and utter contempt for what the future might bring forth.

We looked back even at that moment with an eager longing towards the wilderness of prairies and mountains behind us. For myself I had suffered more that summer from illness than ever before in my life, and yet to this hour I cannot recall those savage scenes and savage men without a strong desire again to visit them.

These romantic passages are undigested rhetoric which, if a means could be found to include them, would have altered the tone of *The Oregon Trail*. They hint at the peculiar quality of the Western experience. That much, at any rate, has been lost in the transformation from West to East — yet these passages were, after all, in the *Knickerbocker*, whose editor's program was to "contribute to the pleasant, *enjoyable* spirits of our readers. . . . We shall save them from politics and polemics. No man shall be deified or diabolized on our pages."[15]

I am, therefore, inclined to dismiss the summary judgment of Mason Wade: "Still more of the original quality was lost by the editing of Charles Eliot Norton, who revised the *Knickerbocker* version for book publication in accordance with the literary amenities as then understood by right-

[15] "Editor's Table," *Knickerbocker Magazine*, XXIX (June, 1847), 579.

thinking Bostonians. . . . [*The Oregon Trail*] was carefully
bowldlerized of much anthropological data and many in-
sights into Western life which seemed too crude to his [Nor-
ton's] delicate taste." [16]

   The major transformation is, of course, in the writing of the
Knickerbocker episodes from the basis of the journal, and it
is this which Doughty and Wade have considered in detail.
Parkman's problem, like Flint's or Irving's, was to transform
a journal into literature without losing the sharpness of impression of the journal: the "crisp, incisive vernacular" could
be lost in the "somewhat formal, 'mandarin' English" of the
period.[17] Doughty makes the point that the *depth* of the book
more than compensates for the loss of freshness. The *shaping*
into book form, however, might involve some distortion;
Doughty's study does not find this true: "the journals, to repeat, can hardly be said to reveal any major distortion of emphasis between the day-to-day records of the experience and
their final reworking in the shape of a narrative of travel." [18]
Such distortion is evident in Irving's *Tour*; it is not evident
in Parkman. Parkman, after all, did not intend to write about
Manifest Destiny or the emigrants on the Oregon Trail. As
he says in his book, "I had come into the country chiefly with
a view of observing the Indian character." As he says with
greater emphasis in the *Knickerbocker* version: "I had come
into the country almost exclusively with a view of observing
the Indian character. Having from childhood felt a curiosity
on this subject, and having failed completely to gratify it by
reading, I resolved to have resource to observation. I wished
to satisfy myself with regard to the position of Indians among
the races of men; the vices and virtues that have sprung from
their innate character and from their modes of life, their government, their superstitions and their domestic situation." Giv-
en that base, there is no distortion of history in the writing up

[16] Wade, *Journals*, II, 387.
[17] Doughty, p. 152.
[18] *Ibid.*, p. 151.

in a literary form. And as we have seen, documentation alone will not keep alive the sense of the past.

But it is in comparison with Irving that we can best estimate the quality of the style of *The Oregon Trail*. Both Irving and Parkman suffer from the limitations of their training. The Western people that they wrote about had to be represented in gentlemanly terms — to coin a word, de-vernacularized. Parkman uses conversation liberally in his book, but he is usually as stilted as was Irving:

"What is that black spot out there on the prairie?"
"It looks like a dead buffalo," answered Raymond.

This passage serves only as a transition from one episode to another, a device to save time in getting from place to place. It could have been written by Irving. On another approach Parkman has Reynal say: "'Come on! come on!' he called to us. 'Do you see that band of big-horn up yonder? If there's one of them, there's a hundred!'" Now, although he has gone beyond Irving's greater formality, Parkman still has a stiffness in the vernacular such that it remains lifeless — simply arranged — as compared to the much more realistic conversation quoted earlier from the journal. But the level of the sound of people to which Parkman could not reach and didn't even try is indicated in such a sentence as this: "There was a burst of screams and laughter from all the women, in which his mistress herself took part, and Raymond was assailed by such a shower of witticisms that he was glad to ride forward out of hearing." For the literature we seek, such a lively scene must be represented in more lively terms than these.

The Western landscape about which Parkman wrote is treated exactly as Irving treated it: the word "picturesque" is used as frequently in Parkman as in Irving — and I use it here in its damning sense of being inanimate, two-dimensional, and simply pretty. A quotation from the *Knickerbocker* version is instructive: "When our grim old tree, lighted by the horizontal rays, assumed an aspect of peaceful repose, such as the soul loves after scenes of tumult and excitement;

and when the whole wild landscape, of swelling plains and scattered groves, was softened into a tranquil beauty; then our encampment presented a striking spectacle. Could Salvator Rosa have transferred it to his canvas, it would have added new renown to his pencil." The lines could have been written by Irving. A writer does not reach to the heights of literature by passing his description problem off in terms of a second-rate painter. This picture is on the level of the "quiet student of belles-lettres" which Parkman had been before his Western trip. *The Oregon Trail* is, indeed, no better stylistically than his first *Knickerbocker* sketches of 1844.

The tone is a kind of *Weltschmerz*, the pose of a man who sits on a buffalo skull only to remember New England. Its source is understandable. We must remember the young man after his incredible journey, forced to endure the darkened room of a sanitarium, half afraid of the turmoil in his brain, suffering hourly pain and dejection, and recalling almost as if to preserve his sanity *pictures* of the West. The confines of Parkman's literature can only loosely be ascribed to the East; they are the confines of that darkened room which he tried to make radiant with the remembered freedom of the West. One senses in *The Oregon Trail* Parkman's consciousness of something lost, of something which he verged on but did not actually touch — conscious of his own peripheral status — and the consequent longing, the mythic pull. Possibly, too, one can read in the book the despair of the Easterner unable to find in his own past the means to express what he so vaguely understands.

> A mind not to be chang'd by place or time,
> The mind is its own place, and in itself
> Can make a heaven of hell, a hell of heaven.

That quality in Parkman is very Eastern indeed.

It is ironic that this ailing Easterner should become the greatest of all the historians of the American Indian, of the myriad tribes who, until Parkman, had no means of survival in the written word. It is ironic too that this rich young sportsman with his scorn of the emigrants should write the most enduring record of the emigrants on the Oregon Trail. Nothing I have said above is intended to belittle that very fine accomplishment. But this was 1849. In that year Sam Clemens, age thirteen, published two humorous poems in the Hannibal *Missouri Courier*, his first known appearance in print. Considering the time and place — so distant from the ties to the East — perhaps he will be able to contain the West, that symbol of freedom which to Parkman had been only the agony and anguish of desire.

5

FROM WEST TO EAST: Mark Twain

He was not from the West at all. Like his predecessors who wrote about the West, he was raised in the eastern half of the nation and went west as a tourist — peripatetic — never staying in one location more than a year, probably never intending to do more than get rich and get out, his eyes fixed on the East from the time he was seventeen on. For he had gone east first in 1853, before his eighteenth birthday. He went alone, running away from home in the sense of leaving Hannibal, ostensibly to try for a better job in St. Louis but in reality leaving home with the secret intent of going on to New York. When he went west eight years later, it was because his occupation had been cut off by national events and because he had had enough of the Civil War in his few weeks of militia experience; he headed west at the first opportunity. He spent just over five years there — the war years and one more — and when he had found an occupation which would pay him better than river-boat piloting had paid he went east again, going back west just once more, briefly, in 1868, on business, and then staying in the East for good. Twain in the

West was like a carpetbagger in the South or like a traveling salesman looking for a new territory — nothing more significant than that.

This uncanonical reading of Twain, this point of view, belittles the contrasts in Henry Seidel Canby's *Turn East, Turn West* and glosses over the whole troublesome controversy between Van Wyck Brooks and Bernard DeVoto about the relative value of Twain's Western experiences.[1] So much critical writing has been done on this subject that one is tempted to quote Twain's "Persons attempting to find a motive in this narrative will be prosecuted," avoid trouble, and close up the books. And yet this point of view of Twain as a mere tourist might be revealing — to place Twain alongside Flint or Irving tells us something immediately — and it may be worth while to go over once again that whole fantastic story of Twain's life (the story of America's life), in search of the significance to him of the environments of his youth.

The point of departure is to insist that Hannibal is in the East, or at least that it is not in the West or Southwest. Geographically, the Mississippi River separates East and West with its broad kris, but the valley is related to the East in its forest cover, its agriculture, and its pattern of settlement. In the pre-1850 period the main lines of communication and travel were by water, south to New Orleans or east along the Ohio to Cincinnati, quite counter to the future cross-country westward movement. A cultural map would swing Hannibal down to St. Louis and both down to Cairo, Illinois, so that the new location would better approximate the Mason-Dixon line; then the alliances would show as divided between North and South, more to the South than to the North, but to both as aspects of what we think of in terms of the East. The West as a separate geography begins, as we have seen, somewhere along

[1] Henry Seidel Canby, *Turn East, Turn West* (Boston: Houghton Mifflin, 1951); Van Wyck Brooks, *The Ordeal of Mark Twain,* revised edition (New York: Dutton, 1933); Bernard DeVoto, *Mark Twain's America* (Boston: Little, Brown, 1932).

the western border of Missouri or on the line of the 100th meridian or even farther west. Call the Mississippi valley a separate culture or call it a part of the East; but don't think of Hannibal in terms of the West. That backwater, slave-holding, decelerating community was nowhere near the West. Thus, Sam Clemens did not enter the West until July 26, 1861, when the stage for Nevada Territory set out from St. Joseph, Missouri, and by then Clemens was twenty-five years old.

If you would argue that the West is a floating term depend-ent on the moving line of the frontier, then my point is re-inforced. The frontier by the beginning of Sam Clemens' awareness (say 1850, when Sam was fourteen) was already west of Hannibal. The frontier is commonly defined as the line drawn through regions with a population of two to six inhabitants per square mile; that line in 1850 cut across cen-tral Iowa and western Missouri.[2] In reality, the westward-moving frontier line intercepted and jumped over an area of far prior settlement in the river towns of the Mississippi and the Missouri: lead mines near Dubuque, Iowa, were worked by 1788; the naming of St. Louis dates back to 1764. The river towns were older by far than the inland towns on the frontier. Hannibal had been there since 1819, had a popula-tion of over 1,000 in 1840, and was by then "a miniature porkopolis, cigar manufactory, whisky distillery, and impor-tant river port for Northern Missouri,"[3] before Sam Clemens was out of diapers. Hannibal was neither in the West nor, in Clemens' time, on the frontier. Provincial it certainly was, and certainly there were successive waves of frontiers, stages of civilization, but the vast empty land — in Twain's term, "the Territory" — was by his time farther west.

And by the time Sam was seventeen, Hannibal was a good

[2] See, for example, William J. Petersen, "Frontiers of the Pioneers," *The Palimpsest*, XXXII (January, 1951), 55–56; see also Paul J. Carter, Jr., "The Influence of the Nevada Frontier on Mark Twain," *Western Humanities Review*, XIII (Winter, 1959), 61–62.

[3] Dixon Wecter, *Sam Clemens of Hannibal* (Boston: Houghton Mifflin, 1952), p. 57. Wecter's work is the primary source of bio-graphical information on Twain to 1853.

place to be *from*. The action was somewhere else. Hannibal's name and its hopes were as farfetched as those of the miniscule Pacific City, Iowa; by 1853 Hannibal's population was draining west, and its backwater destiny was clear. The Hannibal newspaper recorded the westward excitement at a time when the typesetter, copy boy, and prentice printer was young Sam Clemens. The preceding few years (more definitely, the years in Hannibal and the summers on the Quarles farm before the beginning of Sam's newspaper apprenticeship in 1848 — it is significant that Twain did not look back with joy on his five-year period of work after 1848) would turn out to have been the apex of his existence, the source of his only great writing, the idyll (the term is DeVoto's) of nineteenth-century America. But from the point of view of Hannibal and the age of seventeen, none of this could be predicted. The important thing was to get clear, to get shut of the restrictions of home and Orion — to be free.

But by no logic could he have gone west. The Clemens family and related clan out of Tennessee had come to a dead halt in the Mississippi valley; without kin, a boy of seventeen could hardly go west alone. Sam Clemens was educated enough and civilized enough and urban enough and poor enough and just skilled enough in a trade so that once he left the family board he had to go to urban centers to better himself. One must realize, for example, that the Virginia City *Territorial Enterprise* would not be founded until 1858, and that when Sam left Hannibal, San Francisco was smaller than St. Louis and both were smaller than Cincinnati, in order to see the cold logic of Sam's counter-American movement. Sam Clemens was not yet Huck Finn, ready to light out for the Territory. Sam must have wanted the bourgeois comforts which Tom Sawyer so enjoyed. *The Adventures of Huckleberry Finn* is in part a yearning for the complete freedom that Sam Clemens never had.

Nor could he at the age of seventeen sustain himself by writing (and not until nine years more had passed). The few

squibs he wrote in 1852 or 1853 for Orion's newspaper were
not worth a cent in hard cash. True, there were around forty
items, including sentimental poetry, hoaxes, satires, village
gossip, and one decent sketch, "The Dandy Frightening the
Squatter," and certainly these served as a gun aiming the
later Mark Twain in a certain unswerving stylistic direction;
but in 1853 these were no more than the idle pastimes of a
substitute juvenile editor, the work of a typesetter left alone
for a time in the shop. And so, when Orion returned, Sam left,
telling his mother he would find a job in St. Louis where he
would be safely cared for by his sister Pamela Moffett (who
had so luckily married into money), but going there only long
enough to get the money to go on.

Paine's version of Orion's journal puts a telling emphasis
on the economic Horatio Alger–like departure: "'And so,' Orion records, 'he went wandering in search of that comfort and
that advancement and those rewards of industry which he
had failed to find where I was — gloomy, taciturn, and sel-
fish. I not only missed his labor; we all missed his bounding
activity and merriment.'"[4] (It is interesting that it was Sam's
departure in 1853, not the death of the father in 1847, that
broke up the Hannibal home. Orion could not maintain the
newspaper; he took the rest of the Clemens family upriver to
Muscatine, Iowa, late in 1853.)

The significant point is that Sam went east alone and that
he failed, and that, when he came back, his home had vanished.

And yet, how much do we really know about this period of
Twain's life? The *Wanderjahr* lasted from about May, 1853,
to the summer of 1854, and included stops at St. Louis, New
York, Philadelphia, and Washington. On his return Sam visited briefly in Muscatine and then spent about half a year with
a St. Louis newspaper. Early in 1855 Sam moved to Keokuk,
Iowa (where the newly married Orion had gone in order to

[4] Albert Bigelow Paine, *Mark Twain: A Biography* (3 vols.; New
York: Harper, 1912), I, 93.

set up a print shop), and lived there until November, 1856. Then he worked for a printer in Cincinnati until April, 1857, the beginning date of his new life as a river-boat pilot. These make four years, the equivalent of a college career. Is it conceivable that the novice writer did not write in this period? As far as we know, he wrote only letters home; some of these were published in the Hannibal *Journal* or as "Correspondence" in the Muscatine *Journal*; three travel letters by Thomas Jefferson Snodgrass were published in the Keokuk *Daily Post* and the Keokuk *Saturday Post*.[5] The totals:

late 1853	9 items
1854	1 item
1855	2 items
1856	5 items
early 1857	1 item

Continue the tabulation into the river-boat period, April, 1857, through the spring of 1861, remembering that the ten Quintus Curtius Snodgrass letters in the New Orleans *Crescent* of 1861 are only attributed to Clemens: [6]

late 1857	1 item
1858	3 items
1859	3 items
1860	3 items
early 1861	12 items

That makes eight years, graduate school on top of college, about which we know next to nothing. The river-boat years are, of course, recalled in *Life on the Mississippi*, but the *Wanderjahr* and the Iowa years were never recalled specifically in print. At least two scholars, Branch and Lorch, have searched the Muscatine papers and found nothing more which

[5] My figures are taken from E. M. Branch, "A Chronological Bibliography of the Writings of Samuel Clemens to June 8, 1867," *American Literature*, XVIII (May, 1946), 109–159.

[6] The latest discussion concludes that Twain did not write them: Allen Bates, "The Quintus Curtius Snodgrass Letters: A Clarification of the Mark Twain Canon," *American Literature*, XXXVI (March, 1964), 31–37.

can be attributed to Clemens,[7] for unsigned articles or pen names were the rule in facetious writing of the period. Nevertheless, the suspicion remains that Clemens could have written any number of items in the period, items which could have been borrowed by any newspaper in the country.[8] The paucity of Clemens' writing in the years 1853–61 may mean only that our literary scholarship is faulty, though of course it may mean that Clemens was not writing anything. Lacking more evidence, critics make much of the Muscatine or the New Orleans Snodgrass letters, lest they have on their hands in 1862 a full-blown humorist on the *Territorial Enterprise*; yet it is worth underlining here that we know *next to nothing* of the preceding years.

The few letters of 1853–54 contain a very pedestrian writing, some of it, indeed, compiled from a guidebook of Philadelphia.[9] It is obvious that Sam was awed by the cities of the East and also that he was homesick as early as December, 1853, but too poor to pay his fare back home.[10] (Yet he had written Orion in October, "'Down-hearted,' the devil! I have not had a particle of such a feeling since I left Hannibal more than four months ago."[11]) In the summer of 1854 Sam returned, but there was no *reason* for him to return, no home, no home town. His mother was about to be installed with

[7] Edgar M. Branch, *The Literary Apprenticeship of Mark Twain* (Urbana: University of Illinois Press, 1950); Fred W. Lorch, "Mark Twain in Iowa," *Iowa Journal of History and Politics*, XXVII (July, 1929), 408–456.

[8] An item on "Western Eloquence" in the Nevada City, California, *Nevada Democrat*, July 24, 1862, is cited as material which could have been written by Twain; see Paul Fatout, *Mark Twain in Virginia City* (Bloomington: Indiana University Press, 1964), pp. 5–6. The item is similar to an editorial in the Sioux City, Iowa, *Eagle*, August 27, 1859; see my article "Politics and Society in Sioux City, 1859," *Iowa Journal of History*, LIV (April, 1956), 129–130.

[9] Fred W. Lorch, "Mark Twain's Philadelphia Letters in the Muscatine *Journal*," *American Literature*, XVII (January, 1946), 348–351.

[10] Albert Bigelow Paine, ed., *Mark Twain's Letters* (2 vols.; New York: Harper, 1917), I, 30.

[11] *Ibid.*, I, 27.

Pamela in St. Louis. Orion's print shop in Keokuk was going steadily downhill. But Sam joined the menage, rooming with his younger brother Henry in the print shop office, spending most of his time complaining about Orion's disorderly business, and dreaming about an escape to South America. About the Iowa period we know little more. From any point of view it was a stagnation and inaction at a time of maturation when we would most expect a fever of activity. Keokuk, like Hannibal, was a good place to be *from*.

Part of the Twain legend is that a November wind blew a $50 bill into his path, and that through this piece of luck Sam was able to break away from Orion. Brazil was in his mind as his destination when he left, presumably for New York as a shipping point. Why, then, did he go only as far as Cincinnati? He spent the winter there working as a printer and in the spring started out again, heading this time downriver for New Orleans. The trip was a turning point, for the river-boat life proved congenial, and Sam began his second apprenticeship (now at the age of twenty-one) in a life seemingly completely removed from his future in writing.

It was life at a new pitch, even if it was still restricted to the valley of the Mississippi. It answered perfectly to Sam Clemens' restlessness and it assured him, too, of stopovers with his family — stops made with money in his pocket and a cigar stuck in the corner of his mouth. We can only guess at what that life meant to him in terms of the drinking, gambling, whoring, and confidence games which were the fringe benefits of such a profession, for Twain himself never mentioned them. The point seems to be that he had a status, a place in a society, and that it satisfied him. Then, abruptly, the Civil War closed the river traffic and left unemployed a man with expensive tastes — a man who could no longer go back to the menial life of a typesetter. With the South cut off and the East in turmoil, where could he go? After an unfortunate brief interlude with the Missouri militia, Sam's out was clear — he headed west.

"We jumped into the stage, the driver cracked his whip, and we bowled away and left 'the States' behind us. It was a superb summer morning, and all the landscape was brilliant with sunshine. There was a freshness and breeziness, too, and an exhilarating sense of emancipation from all sorts of cares and responsibilities, that almost made us feel that the years we had spent in the close, hot city, toiling and slaving, had been wasted and thrown away." [12] The reader will realize that in this quotation from *Roughing It* there are, in the words of Huck Finn, "some stretchers." Clemens had not toiled for years in a close, hot city; but it is certainly true that the trip west was an escape from cares and responsibilities, fitting into the well-established picaresque pattern of his previous life. The trip lasted, all told, five years; and then five more years elapsed before the experiences in the West were published in book form. By then, of course, they had been transformed by the character of a different man — Mark Twain. The rhapsody quoted above came in retrospect, at a later date; for at the time Sam Clemens was incapable of such heady prose. A series of metamorphoses intervened between 1861 and 1872.

Our first knowledge of Clemens in the West — he arrived at Carson City on August 14, 1861 — is in his letters home, and in particular in the one letter to his mother which Clemens revised for publication on October 26, 1861, for the Keokuk *Gate City*. It is evident from the study of these letters made by Franklin R. Rogers [13] that Clemens had never abandoned writing for newspapers, and that his base was the personal letter, a mixture of homesickness and excitement over a new environment, with a braggadocio whose modern equivalent is "Kilroy was here." But such writing was secondary and the product of periodic inactivity. Sam Clemens, like everyone

[12] Mark Twain, *Roughing It*, in *The Writings of Mark Twain*, Author's National Edition (25 vols.; New York: Harper, 1907–18), VII, 18. Future quotations from this text are not footnoted.
[13] Franklin R. Rogers, ed., *The Pattern for Mark Twain's Roughing It* (Berkeley: University of California Press, 1961), pp. 7–12.

else in Nevada Territory, was caught up in the fever of getting rich quick. We can hardly keep track of his ventures: the trip or trips to Lake Tahoe regarding timber land, the trip two hundred miles northeast to the Humboldt Mining District, and another long trip south and east to the Esmeralda Mining District. The few letters of this first year are pathetic in their hypnotized optimism. To Orion, on May 11, 1862: "I have got the thing sifted down to a dead moral certainty. I own one-eighth of the new 'Monitor Ledge, Clemens Company,' and money can't buy a foot of it; because I *know* it to contain our fortune."[14] But even while he wrote this he had been reduced to doing his own pick and shovel work and hiring out as manual labor to get his daily meals.

Some idle letters he had sent to the Virginia City *Territorial Enterprise* (as early as April, 1862, although these letters are not extant[15]) led to the offer of a job as a local reporter at $25 a week — just above the level of subsistence in that inflated community. Sam reluctantly gave up his mining hopes. Perhaps it should be emphasized that in his first year in Nevada Territory he was not waiting eagerly for an opening on a newspaper. His *Enterprise* job was a tremendous comedown from his Mississippi piloting or from his capitalist dreams of the winter of 1861–62. He began his full-time writing career as a last resort, and he signaled the change, acknowledged a new personality, by changing his name. The new name would enable him to look back and down on Sam Clemens as a fool.

Mark Twain stayed in Virginia City some twenty months; rather, that was his home base, for the roving reporter went frequently to Carson City to write up the doings of the territorial legislature, or he took extensive vacations (paid for by his newspaper letters) to San Francisco. In that leisurely posture — "They pay me six dollars a day, and I make 50 per cent profit by only doing three dollars' worth of work"[16] —

[14] *Letters*, I, 73.
[15] Samuel Charles Webster, ed., *Mark Twain, Business Man* (Boston: Little, Brown, 1946), p. 68.
[16] *Ibid.*, p. 77.

amused and superior, he learned the West, absorbing sights and sounds of the frantic activity as no miner, saloon keeper, or lawyer could. Throwing off the shackles of Orion and his family life, Twain lived with a group of newspaper men who acted more like boys than men in their friendly rivalry to see who could write the most outrageous material. He swore, he drank, and no doubt he visited the houses of delight wherever he went. He learned from Dan De Quille and Artemus Ward a humor which was idle, meaningless, mere newspaper filler (and through the urging of Ward, he sent off east a skit on "Those Blasted Children" and was delighted to see it published in the New York *Sunday Mercury*). He dubbed his friend Clement T. Rice of the *Daily Union* "The Unreliable" and wrote witty nothings about his coarse manners: "I must go out now with this conceited ass — there is no other way to get rid of him." [17] All in all he learned, as a contemporary put it, "that shrewd, graceless, good-humored, cynical way of looking at things as they in fact are — unbullied by authority and indifferent to tradition," which critics find as the base of all his best literary work.[18]

Then, drunk one night, he wrote a squib jokingly insulting some ladies of Carson City; but they were not amused, and he had gone too far. The friendly rivalry of other papers became decidedly unfriendly. Twain lashed back, refusing to apologize. Suddenly, in a kind of nightmare, he discovered that he had challenged several men to duels and that they were taking the challenges in dead earnest. Twain and his second, Steve Gillis, abruptly left town on May 29, 1864. It was the end of what he later called the best years of his life.[19]

He might have gone east then, but he was still penniless, and the war was still on. Moreover, he had connections now with newspapers in San Francisco; and it is further obvious that he was by now very much attached to urban amenities.

---

[17] Henry Nash Smith and Frederick Anderson, eds., *Mark Twain of the Enterprise* (Berkeley: University of California Press, 1957), p. 65.

[18] *Ibid.*, p. 30.

[19] The episode is told best and at length in Fatout, pp. 196–215.

San Francisco was a far cry from Virginia City, and the Hannibal origin receded further into the background: "To a Christian who has toiled months and months in Washoe; whose hair bristles from a bed of sand, and whose soul is caked with a cement of alkali dust; whose nostrils know no perfume but the rank odor of sage-brush — and whose eyes know no landscape but barren mountains and desolate plains; where the winds blow, and the sun blisters, and the broken spirit of the contrite heart finds joy and peace only in Limberger cheese and lager beer — unto such a Christian, verily, the Occidental Hotel is Heaven on the half shell." [20]

But his job, as a city reporter on the San Francisco *Call*, lacked interest. Twain found it drudgery, and it comes as no surprise to find him restlessly writing home on September 25, 1864, "But I need a change and must move again." [21] Probably in October he was fired from the *Call*. Then Steve Gillis got into trouble with the police; Mark Twain posted bond for him, and both left town. Steve went back to Virginia City and Mark went to a kind of Bohemian existence with Steve's brother Jim in a cabin in the Tuolumne Hills; and it was that winter that he heard a former river pilot drone out a laconic tale about a jumping frog.

By the end of February, 1865, Twain was back in San Francisco, still too impoverished to go home, but able now to sustain himself by free-lance contributions to newspapers and to journals like the literary *Golden Era*.[22] We know little about his next year, but note that he was able to sit still for just that one year. For he still lacked, and did not know it, respectability. He really had no drive, no future, no reason to write; he had passed the level of his humorist competitors and did not know where to go from there. He was now, in 1866, thirty

[20] Franklin Walker, ed., *The Washoe Giant in San Francisco* (San Francisco: G. Fields, 1938), pp. 74–75.

[21] Paine, *Mark Twain*, I, 256.

[22] A new selection of Twain's writings during the San Francisco period is in Bernard Taper, ed., *Mark Twain's San Francisco* (New York: McGraw-Hill, 1963).

years old — too far from his old home to go back and still
with no prospect of founding a home of his own. His rich tastes
were still beyond his means. His motivations were still those
of an adventurer, an opportunist, an inveterate wanderer,
living from day to day. In the East he was known, but not
widely known, as a humorist — primarily on the basis of the
one jumping frog story, first published in the New York *Saturday Press* of November 18, 1865. In the West he was known
for innumerable newspaper skits and for the "letters home"
— the medium for his exaggerated tales of the wonders of the
Western man. And though with Bret Harte he had vague
ideas of publishing his sketches in book form, the more
typical mood is that of a letter of January 20, 1866, "I do not
know what to write; my life is so uneventful." [23]

And so, when the first passenger steamers began the Sandwich Island trade, Twain maneuvered a commission to write
letters back to the Sacramento *Weekly Union* in the seven-
month period beginning in March, 1866. To be paid for traveling — this must have been the apex of his ambition at the
time. There were twenty-five letters. We shall look at them in
the later context of *Roughing It* and note here only the spas-
modic mention of an uncouth friend, Mr. Brown, based on no
particular person but an obvious extension of "the Unreliable"
of Virginia City days. This *persona*, to use the term of Henry
Nash Smith,[24] is an alter ego of Twain, an earlier Twain or
Clemens in contrast to the changing man who was increasingly identifying himself with the business community. Twain
himself and his critics made much of the advice given him on
this trip by Anson Burlingame (on his way to his post as minister to China): "What you need now is the refinement of
association. Seek companionship among men of superior intellect and character. Refine yourself and your work. Never
affiliate with inferiors; always climb." [25] Brown was the de-

[23] Paine, *Mark Twain*, I, 278.
[24] Henry Nash Smith, *Mark Twain, The Development of a Writer*
(Cambridge, Massachusetts: Belknap Press, 1962), p. vii ff.
[25] Paine, *Mark Twain*, I, 287.

vice by which he could objectify and refine away his character of the past.

The next adventure is well known: the rediscovery of his ability to give humorous lectures (he had done this as early as the Keokuk days of 1855–56 and again in Virginia City in 1862–63) and the startling discovery that this was at last the means by which he could live in style. The October 2, 1866, lecture in San Francisco led to a tour of other California towns and into Nevada for a triumphant return to Virginia City. And after that and at last, the return to the East.

Twain insured his solvency by a commission for more travel letters, twenty-six of them, this time to the San Francisco *Alta California,* and he left San Francisco (accompanied by his mythical friend Brown) on December 15, 1866. He sailed via Nicaragua and arrived in New York on January 11, 1867. The move from the West to the East was accomplished physically, but it would take some time before it would be accomplished spiritually as well. He had to get rid of Brown.

There is no need here to do more than make note of the eastern hegiras of the next two years. Plans were made for the publication on May 1, 1867, of the Western materials as *The Celebrated Jumping Frog of Calaveras County and Other Sketches.* Plans were made for a book on the Sandwich Islands — and temporarily discarded. Plans were made for a trip around the world — and discarded. Twain made a trip "home" to St. Louis and Keokuk and gave lectures there, followed by a lecture in New York. He contracted with the *Alta California* and with the New York *Tribune* for more travel letters, and spent June 8 to November 19, 1867, on the *Quaker City* excursion to the Holy Land. After a brief, abortive experience in Washington, D.C., as secretary to Senator William M. Stewart of Nevada, Twain went back to New York in December for a fateful first meeting with Olivia Langdon, such that the next year, 1868, was consumed in the activity of becoming respectable enough to become engaged to her. He wrote and lectured. The engagement was announced on February 4, 1869, and the publication of *The Innocents Abroad* took place on July 20, 1869. Twain's future was thus secured.

The process of *civilizing* Twain, which went into the writing of *The Innocents Abroad,* was a part of his move from West to East and deserves to be spelled out in some detail. It was part and parcel of his need to be accepted into the bourgeois household of the Elmira coal merchant Jervis Langdon (who was to respond so graciously by giving Twain his daughter, a furnished house, and a third interest in the Buffalo *Express*—shackles enough for any man).

Twain's fifty letters to the *Alta California* and six letters to the *Tribune* appear to have been written spasmodically, governed by the deadlines of homeward-bound, mail-carrying ships (twenty-eight letters are dated from June through August, twenty-seven letters are dated September, one in October, and two more in November). Twain therefore kept a journal of impressions, expanding sentences at a later date to paragraphs, paragraphs to complete letters. The published journal, edited by Albert Bigelow Paine, was bowdlerized.[26] The original journal is in the Mark Twain Papers at Berkeley, complete save for the period of travel between Tangiers and Naples, a period of about a month. Sketchy as the journal is, it is the writing of an unreformed Twain. His fictitious friend Brown is there, as Dixon Wecter notes, "a congeries of offensive odors, symptoms, and regurgitations."[27] The language and observations are roughhewn. A character is quoted as saying, "Stop the boat you old pot-b—— son of a b——," and religion is treated lightheartedly: "Looks like he is waiting for a vacancy in the Trinity."[28] I judge this journal to be only a little more offensive (and that is certainly not very offensive by our standards) than the previous series of letters to the *Alta California* on the voyage from San Francisco to New York. But when Twain came to write the new series of letters, he refined his journal. Wecter notes that Twain was always his

[26] Dixon Wecter, ed., *The Letters of Mark Twain to Mrs. Fairbanks* (San Marino, California: Huntington Library, 1949), p. xxiv.

[27] *Ibid.*

[28] *Ibid.*, pp. xxiv–xxv.

own "most attentive censor in writing for the general public" [29] and also that he was now under the influence of a Mrs.
Mary Mason Fairbanks, who acted as a second censor. A
passenger on the *Quaker City* remembered Twain tearing
up a manuscript with the comment, "Mrs. Fairbanks thinks
it oughtn't to be printed, and like as not she is right." [30] This
remarkable woman undertook to civilize Twain as a writer
and as a person, and he loved her for it. She was thirty-nine
(Twain, thirty-one), aggressively educated, married to the
wealthy publisher of the Cleveland *Herald*, a man twelve
years her senior. In the hallowed *Quaker City* atmosphere no
affair would have been possible, even if probable; but Mrs.
Fairbanks, traveling alone, was midway between the saintly
elderly majority on the ship and the more vivacious, younger
minority; her own independent spirit would lean toward
Twain's. Moreover, she was a correspondent to her husband's
newspaper and considered Twain as a fellow journalist. Her
own work was "well-written but guide-bookish," [31] and she
took it upon herself to correct Twain's native bent.

Her influence would be gradual and it certainly was not
all-pervasive at first. Mrs. Fairbanks did not censor, for example, the mention of a bawdy house in the *Alta* letter #10,
nor the skit on nude bathing in #21, nor the mention of
water closets in #29 (dated September 17, 1867), but the
second half of the *Alta* letters seems to me to contain fewer
censorable items than the first half. However, her influence
was more pervasive when Twain came to write *The Innocents Abroad*. It appears that by December, 1867, Mrs. Fairbanks had extracted from Twain a promise *not* to write, as
Twain said, "the savagest kind of history of the excursion"
which he felt like doing. [32]

But other censors began to operate before he finished his
book. In January, 1868, Twain visited for the first time — and
fell in love with — the Nook Farm circle at Hartford, and

[29] *Ibid.*, p. xxv.
[30] *Ibid.*, p. xxiv.
[31] *Ibid.*, p. xxi.
[32] *Ibid.*, p. 4.

wrote to Mrs. Fairbanks, "I desire to have the respect of this
sterling old Puritan community, for their respect is worth
having." [33] And by February Twain could write to Mrs. Fairbanks: "No, I don't need a guardian *now*, because I am re-
formed, now — I have finished up since I wrote last. . . .
Unless I get too much pushed for time I think I will write
almost the entire book new — I don't like *any* of those letters
that have reached me from California so far. I may think better of those you weeded of slang, though. There will not be
any slang in this book except it should occur in a mild form in
dialogues." [34] For of course by this time he had begun to woo
that other censor, Olivia Langdon. The *Alta* letters would
have to be purged.

There is no question but that *The Innocents Abroad* makes
a better book than the *Alta* letters; critics agree on the tighter
structure, the improved diction, the clarity of expression, and
a decorum such that the book was "funny without being vulgar" (Twain apparently is quoting the dictum of Mrs. Fairbanks). [35] But the specific changes made are highly instructive:

Alta letter	*The Innocents Abroad*
the first pass we made	the first adventure we made
leaving it to others to cipher out	leaving it to others to determine
seedy rascal	vagabond
I coppered the statement	I doubted
roped in	deceived
spit across	almost jump across
green	inexperienced
forty-horse team of lazy priests	battalions of priests
monuments of human folly	church edifices
cheek	effrontery
loafing in Paradise and hobnobbing	seated in heaven and conversing
brutes	miscreants
corral all the people	assemble all the people
browse around among	go among
the crowd of staring asses	the crowd

[33] *Ibid.*, p. 15.
[34] *Ibid.*, pp. 21–22.
[35] *Ibid.*, p. 18.

tom-foolery	excitement
scoundrel	vagrant
I reckon	I suppose
has got a good thing	has got a fortune
stand any show	provoke any notice
take a drink	converse
blow-out	luncheon
figure it out	determine
ante up and pass the buck	die
stretched	exaggerated
closed out	destroyed
sweating for it	suffering for it
gotten up	invented
strong suit	specialty
squirt	discharge
buzzard roost	town
was prospecting here	was here
any of the breed	any of them
cleared out	went away

Arranged thus in columns (and the list of changes could be extended), the civilizing process is evident, and with it a distinctive loss of quality. The language in *The Innocents Abroad* is less vivid, less individual, and obviously culled of those terms which originated in either the West or in the gambling saloons of Mississippi steamboats. Twain changed "makes his breath smell like the sigh of a buzzard" to "makes his breath bad." He changed "she had a run of luck the like of which was never seen before nor since" to "was always fortunate." He changed "slimy cesspool that lives in history as the Blessed Pool of Bethesda" to "historic pool of Bethesda." He changed the highly descriptive "had much shekels, and lived in a two-story house and put on more style than any man in Damascus" to "lived in great state." [36] I had thought

[36] The *Alta* quotations are from Samuel Langhorne Clemens, *Traveling with the Innocents Abroad*, Daniel M. McKeithan, ed. (copyright 1958 by the University of Oklahoma Press, Norman). See also Mark Twain, *The Innocents Abroad*, in *The Writings of Mark Twain*, vols. I–II. Future quotations from these texts are not footnoted. See also Leon T. Dickinson, "Mark Twain's Revisions in Writing *The Innocents Abroad*," *American Literature*, XIX (May, 1947), 139–157.

the charm of *The Innocents Abroad* lay in part in the innocence of its narrator and in his use of language; but I find
such naiveté has been de-emphasized in the desire to please
Mrs. Fairbanks, Nook Farm, and Olivia Langdon. The move
from West to East involved a decided change in style.

Change is evident too in the character of young Mr. Blucher in *The Innocents Abroad*, the purged version of Mr. Brown.
He is "from the Far West," but the locale is meaningless. He
is a rube, an innocent, confused by the changes in time zones,
querulous as to what were the symptoms of seasickness ("He
found out"), appalled by foreign currencies, curious about
the insides of mosques, an avid collector of souvenir rocks,
and that is about all. Blucher is a far cry from the Mr. Brown
of the *Alta* letters of the trip from San Francisco to New York:
Brown described with glee the rage of a father whose daughter of fifteen had just married; Brown swore "a chapter of
blasphemy"; he gossiped viciously ("She calls it cologne, you
know, but it's gin"); he ogled native girls in Nicaragua; he
got involved in a string of horses crossing the isthmus, a comic
picture climaxed by his swearing; he drank brandy in a saloon
and spread false rumors of cholera; he wrote in his journal of
a female passenger who picked her nose with a fork; and he
expressed a mere annoyance with a lively relish — "I want to
make trouble: I want to do something that's outrageous. I
want to set a house a-fire — I want to start a riot." [37] Most critics of Twain are not sorry to see the uncouth Mr. Brown dis-
appear and be replaced by Mr. Blucher, but there is an obvious lack of realism in the transformation.

The Innocents Abroad might well be described in terms of
innocence threatened by realism and of a retreating behind
nostalgia. The narrator Twain is keenly aware of his own
naiveté, of the childlike thrill of seeing and doing new things.
"There was that rare thing, novelty, about it; it was a fresh,
new exhilarating sensation, this donkey riding, and worth a
hundred worn and threadbare home pleasures." "A strange,

[37] These quotations are from Franklin Walker and G. Ezra Dane,
eds., *Mark Twain's Travels with Mr. Brown* (New York: Knopf, 1940).

new sensation is a rare thing in this humdrum life, and I had it here." "To do something, say something, see something, before *anybody* else — these are the things that confer a pleasure compared to which other pleasures are tame and commonplace, other ecstacies cheap and trivial." This is one mood of the book, this freshness of impression with Twain groping for the unique and vivid and individual phrase — "The scene is lively, is picturesque, and smells like a police court." But a second mood of *The Innocents Abroad* is one of disillusion. In Europe Twain saw clearly for the first time the twin evils of theocracy and poverty: "We were in the heart and home of priestcraft — of a happy, cheerful, contented ignorance, superstition, degredation, poverty, indolence, and everlasting, unaspiring worthlessness." "Their hungry eyes and their lank forms continually suggested one glaring, unsentimental fact — they wanted what they term in California 'a square meal.'" The "unsentimental fact" is notable, for Twain is alternating between romanticism and realism, well aware that he is choosing between two approaches.

Two noteworthy examples support this, the first the Turkish Bath Fraud. Twain claims to have dreamed for years of the wonders of a Turkish bath, based on impressions garnered from travel books. But "It was a poor miserable imposture." The attendants in the bath were not "a gang of naked savages" but were "cadaverous, half-nude varlets." The pallet he was placed on was, apparently, out of "negro quarters of Arkansas" and "not made of cloth of gold." He was swabbed with a horsetail, dried with a tablecloth, and left to rest in a chicken coop. He concludes that any man who can enjoy this can "enjoy anything that is repulsive to sight or sense, and he that can invest it with a charm of poetry is able to do the same with anything else in the world that is tedious, and wretched, and dismal, and nasty." Romance has been forcibly reduced to an earthy, homely reality. Twain enjoyed a second occasion for rage when considering the travel books of one William C. Grimes (the name he gave to William C. Prime, author of *Tent Life in the Holy Land*, 1857). Grimes had prepared

Twain for bloodthirsty Bedouins, but Twain found they were a fraud — he could outrun them. As to the scenery in Palestine, a Grimesian writer had written, "Of the beauty of the scene I cannot say enough," but the reality to Twain was "an unobtrusive basin of water, some mountainous desolation, and one tree." Thus, to the school of such writers, Twain charges: "But why should not the truth be spoken of this region? Is the truth harmful? Has it ever needed to hide its face? God made the Sea of Galilee and its surroundings as they are. Is it the province of Mr. Grimes to improve upon the work?" Twain is clearly on the side of the realists in this second mood, but by the end of the book he can write this significant passage: "Our experiences in Europe have taught us that in time this fatigue will be forgotten; the heat will be forgotten; the thirst, the tiresome volubility of the guide, the persecutions of the beggars — and then, all that will be left will be pleasant memories of Jerusalem, memories we shall call up with always increasing interest as the years go by, memories which some day will become all beautiful when the last annoyance that incumbers them shall have faded out of our minds never again to return." Twain has discovered a simple fact, that the mind remembers pleasant experiences more readily than unpleasant experiences, that a fact recalled is better than the fact itself. Thus, in a third mood of nostalgia he can now look back in 1869 on that trip west of 1861 and write a perfectly romantic version of the past:

Once I crossed the plains and deserts and mountains of the West, in a stage-coach, from the Missouri line to California, and since then all my pleasure-trips must be measured to that rare holiday frolic. Two thousand miles of ceaseless rush and rattle and clatter, by night and by day, and never a weary moment, never a lapse of interest! The first seven hundred miles a level continent, its grassy carpet greener and softer and smoother than any sea, and figured with designs fitted to its magnitude — the shadows of clouds. Here were no scenes but summer scenes, and no disposition inspired by them but to lie at full length on the mail sacks, in the grateful breeze, and dreamily smoke the pipe of peace — what other, where all was repose and contentment?

And so on. Significantly, this episode, a base of comparison
with railway travel in France, did not appear in the *Alta* letters of 1867. There, French railways are mentioned only in
terms of the station rest rooms: Brown thought all the French
railway stations had the same name, *Côte des Hommes*.

The Innocents Abroad was written, in a manner of speaking, *after* the fall of innocence and from a maturity that
looked back fondly on the past with a readiness to mask whatever was too vivid, too real. Clearly, this is a change in Twain
and can be fixed as occurring between the writing of the *Alta*
letters in 1867 and the publication of *The Innocents Abroad*
in 1869. Twain never finally chose one approach over the
other, the romantic or the realistic—it is the tension between the two which makes his work so interesting—but he
had begun to "civilize" his work in terms of the Eastern
audience for which he was now writing under the dictates
of his own conscience and the criticisms of Mrs. Fairbanks
and Olivia Langdon. Nevertheless, he looked back fondly on
a past which was in part Western (the space, the freedom),
in part rural (Hannibal), in part the simplicity of the pre–
Civil War era, and in part the nostalgia of middle-age, mid-
dle-class sobriety.

The point of view is enlarged and clarified in the writing
of *Roughing It*, the transformation from West to East finally
accomplished in the years 1869-71.

Between Twain's engagement to Olivia Langdon in February, 1869, and the copyright date of December 6, 1871, on
Roughing It, Twain's life became increasingly complex, with
higher peaks and lower depths than he had ever known before. This new period began with a desperate declaration of
independence in a letter to his family, February 27, 1869:

I am particularly anxious to place myself in a position where I can
carry on my married life in good shape on *my own hook*, because
I have paddled my own canoe so long that I could not be satisfied
now to let anybody help me — and my proposed father-in-law is
naturally so liberal that it would be just like him to want to give us

a start in life. But I don't want it that way. I can start myself. I don't want any help. I can run this institution without any outside assistance, and I shall have a wife who will stand by me like a soldier through thick and thin, and never complain.[38]

The protest is feeble, for that summer Twain allowed his future father-in-law to buy him respectability in the form of a partnership on the Buffalo *Express*. However, Twain assumed the $25,000 gift as a debt to be paid off. He went to work for the *Express* on August 14, writing untold quantities of anonymous material,[39] but stopped in October for the more lucrative lecture tour which lasted until his marriage on February 2, 1870. Meanwhile, royalties for *The Innocents Abroad* poured in — supposedly at the rate of $4,000 for a three-month period. In addition, Twain contracted for a monthly column of humor to the New York magazine *The Galaxy* and began contributions with the issue of May, 1870. He also, as we will see, made plans for several books — all of this, apparently, in aspiration to reach the level of Jervis Langdon, whose family expenses, Twain reported, were $40,-000 a year.

Twain's peak was reached in May, 1870, when he could write James Redpath to refuse a lecture tour the next season: "Have got a lovely wife; a lovely house, bewitchingly furnished; a lovely carriage, and a coachman whose style and dignity are simply awe-inspiring — nothing less — and I am making more money than necessary — by considerable, and therefore why crucify myself nightly on the platform." [40]

That month, however, Jervis Langdon had an attack; the whole family nursed him until his death on August 6, 1870. Shortly after that, Olivia's school friend Emma Nye came as a consoling house guest, only to contract typhoid fever and die on September 29. Nursing Emma for more than a month so weakened Olivia that her first child was born prematurely

[38] *Letters*, I, 156–157.
[39] See Henry Duskis, ed., *The Forgotten Writings of Mark Twain* (New York: Philosophical Library, 1963).
[40] *Letters*, I, 172–173.

on November 7, and both mother and child were ill most of the winter. Twain wrote to Orion in March or April of 1871, "My hands are full and more than full." [41] He gave up everything—his house in Buffalo, his interest in the *Express*, his contract with *The Galaxy* — and moved his invalid family in April to the home of Olivia's sister at Quarry Farm, near Elmira, New York.

Since July, 1870, Twain had been trying to write *Roughing It*, but in the depths of the winter had abandoned it.[42] At Quarry Farm in 1871, however, Olivia and the child recuperated quickly, and in a complete reversal of mood Twain wrote his publisher on May 15: "I am writing with a red-hot interest. Nothing grieves me now—nothing troubles me, nothing bothers me or gets my attention—I don't think of anything but the book, and I don't have an hour's unhappiness about anything and don't care two cents whether school keeps or not. It will be a bully book." [43] Clearly the bulk of *Roughing It* was written during that rejuvenating spring in the dominant mood of an escape into a less restrictive past.

Twain had been slow to find his Western subject. He tried first to repeat the *Alta California–The Innocents Abroad* format with a series of "Around the World" letters to the Buffalo *Express*. The letters were to be written jointly by a Professor D. R. Ford (the tutor and traveling companion of Olivia's brother Charles) and by Twain: "The former does the actual traveling, and such facts as escape his notice are supplied by the latter, who remains at home." [44] The collaboration did not work successfully, nor did another collaboration the next year, 1870. Twain prodded his publisher to finance the trip of a California friend J. H. Riley to the diamond fields of South Africa—Twain to enlarge and elaborate Riley's

[41] *Ibid.*, I, 186.

[42] Details of the composition of *Roughing It* are found in Hamlin Hill, *Mark Twain and Elisha Bliss* (Columbia: University of Missouri Press, 1964), pp. 40–54.

[43] *Letters*, I, 187.

[44] Wecter, *Mrs. Fairbanks*, p. 108n.

notes. But Riley died (gruesomely, of blood poisoning, brought on by accidentally stabbing himself with his eating fork) on his way home before anything was written. Another abortive effort was the plan made in the winter of 1869-70 for a fantasy on Noah's Ark — nothing was to come of that for several years. And in the winter of 1870-71 Twain worked up a short and embarrassingly poor book called the (*Burlesque*) *Autobiography and First Romance,* published in February, 1871. Then, sometime in the spring of 1871, he wrote and abandoned a Western drama, planned another long work, and wrote three sketches for the publisher Bliss and three lectures for the forthcoming tour of 1871-72.

So it was at the beginning of this multifarious activity that Bliss suggested, early in 1870, the book which was to become *Roughing It.* Twain had worked fitfully on it in the gloomy summer of 1870 (probably reaching Chapter 7 or 8), broken off, and then continued in March of 1871, going on to finish two-thirds of the book by mid-May, and finishing the book that summer.

Twain collaborated even here. His first step was to ask his mother to send the clippings of his writings for the *Enterprise,* this in March, 1870. Then he asked Orion for his memorandum book which had been kept on the stagecoach trip from Missouri to Nevada in 1861, and was so delighted with it that he agreed to pay Orion $1,000 from his first royalties. Next, he persuaded the former editor of the *Enterprise,* Joe Goodman, to stay with him for perhaps two months in the spring of 1871 to help jog his memory — "[Joe Goodman] writes by my side." [45] Twain also had to draw on his *Express* articles, his letters of 1866 to the Sacramento *Union* on his trip to the Sandwich Islands, and, finally, his successful lecture on the same trip. It was thus to be a work of the scissors and paste pot, and it was to be a travel book — loosely connected sketches and incidents of travel in the genre

[45] Webster, p. 118.

which Twain had already perfected in his newspaper letters, his lectures, and in *The Innocents Abroad.*

And it was written by a man intent on distorting the truth; or, rather, intent on creating truth in his own image. In a prefatory note Twain calls the book a "personal narrative" with the object of helping a reader "while away an idle hour." He apologizes for the "facts" in the book (which, he says, stew up out of him as naturally as "ottar of roses out of the otter") but justifies them on the base that, concerning the silver-mining fever in Nevada, "no books have been written by persons who were on the ground in person, and saw the happenings of the time with their own eyes." Precisely. But the "facts" in the book turn out to be less interesting than the subjective interpretation of the facts; reality will be supplanted regularly by romance.

Roughing It begins in terms of a "long strange journey" into a "curious new world" as seen by a tenderfoot tourist. Orion's notebook is much in evidence in the precise times of departures and arrivals, the daily distance traveled by stage-coach, and Twain adds equally precise descriptions of the way people looked and the way they talked and the way they lived. But he has a penchant for romance. He mimics a boy's thrill at seeing in real life the desperado Slade — and the disappointment at finding Slade so kindhearted and urbane. He looks forward to crossing the Salt Lake desert: "This was fine — novel — romantic — dramatically adventurous — *this*, indeed was worth living for, worth traveling for!" But as it turned out, "the poetry was all in the anticipation — there is none in reality." And later, in the same tone, the Goshoot Indians are presented in disappointing contrast to the expectations aroused in him by Cooper's Red Men. Twain's sympathies seem to be on the side of romance. Along with the comments on the harshness of reality is an exaggeration of fact for comic effect, such as the treatment of the coyote in Chapter 5, or of the buffalo in Chapter 7. The supercilious speed of the one and the ponderous ferocity of the other are so far abstracted from nature itself that they are in no sense real — nor were they intended to be. It was as if, to avoid disappointment, Twain had to populate that empty land with *something*. Is it that the West itself invited such distortion? Perhaps it did; but certainly Twain's coyote is of the same cloth as the mangy dogs in *The Innocents Abroad* — of the author, in other words, not of the setting.

By the time Twain's narrator reaches Carson City in Chapter 21, apparently where Orion's memorandum book source ended, the tone of the book is fixed. Henry Nash Smith speaks of it in terms of the transformation of the tenderfoot into "one of the boys," the acquiring of a superior knowledge through membership in an elite.[46] It was thus apparently part of the game of roughing it not to be concerned by the "solitude, silence, and desolation" (Twain's initial reaction to Carson City), but to see such a reality only in terms of a hilarious exaggeration. We do not need to check back on Twain's own hard-luck experiences to realize that *Roughing It* is a gloss on fact. The middle of the book stems not so much from fact as it does from the habit of newspaper posturing, from "made" news with its exaggerations, hoaxes, satires, witticisms, and burlesques. It is all a pleasantness, all perfectly created in a joyous, sentimental mood of nostalgia. Nor do we need to know that Twain is thirty-five years old and looking back on twenty-five to see the extraction from fact in such lines as those describing the San Francisco population as made up wholly of "stalwart, muscular, dauntless young braves, brimful of push and energy, and royally endowed with every attribute that goes to make up a peerless and magnificent manhood" — "a wild, free, disorderly society!" This is, we realize a hundred years later, the beginning of the myth of the West, false in its dimensions though possibly symbolically true.

The lapse of years between the experience and the writing

[46] Smith, pp. 52–70.

of it — the years of Twain's education in the East — added another specific quality to *Roughing It*, this in the direction of the genteel. As with *The Innocents Abroad* and the letters to the *Alta California*, the last eighteen chapters of *Roughing It* can be compared with their original version in the letters to the Sacramento *Union*.[47] Within the book itself these chapters are clearly inferior to the rest of the book, critics agree, largely because they are not "created"; they are, in fact, an editing job only, done hurriedly and without much thought. The original Sandwich Island letters have been cut down by approximately two-thirds; half of the omissions involve factual exposition, statistics on sugar production, or extraneous matter like the *Hornet* disaster; the other half largely concerns our old friend Brown — completely erased from *Roughing It*.

The material makes, once again, a much tighter narrative in book form, but this time very little work has been done beyond the mechanical slicing. In general, sentence order has not been altered, passages have not been reworked for greater effect. Some few word replacements are made, such as the following:

Union letters	*Roughing It*
raw sores	raw places
one more yarn	one more instance
scoundrel	fellow
venereal disease	certain imported diseases
Lord! how the experiences	How the experiences
fervent curse	left-handed blessing

Thus the changed version is, like *The Innocents Abroad*, a washed and weakened version. And the disreputable, vulgar, dirty, drinking, retching, leering Brown has been thrown out, and with him the revealing comment from the *Alta* letters, "Brown looks at the unpleasant side of everything and I seldom do."

[47] G. Ezra Dane, ed., *Mark Twain's Letters from the Sandwich Islands* (Palo Alto, California: Stanford University Press, 1938). Future quotations from this text are not footnoted.

Quite clearly, Brown was an alter ego of Mark Twain which the latter chose, after 1868, to suppress. Quite possibly the unpleasant Mr. Brown is more realistic, more historically valid than Mark Twain — who was, after all, only a mask for Hannibal's apprentice printer Sam.

Twain's one book on the West (he never reverted to the Western experiences except in the form of sketches and tales) was written from the point of view of Quarry Farm and it was written at a unique time in Twain's life. He had reached the financial goal he had set himself; he had discovered that he was paid highly for writing or lecturing with humor; he had attained marital bliss and an acceptance by the genteel society he had chosen — and disaster had been partner to his success. He recalled in 1906 particularly the days before the death of Emma Nye in September, 1870, as "among the blackest, the gloomiest, the most wretched of my long life," and they were followed by "periodical and sudden changes of mood in me, from deep melancholy to half-insane tempests and cyclones of humor."[48] This is enough to suggest the source of the escapist quality in *Roughing It* — exactly what Twain needed, exactly what makes the book so fine a souvenir of the American past.

From the point of view of the West, however, that quality makes it just another tourist piece, so subjective, so exaggerated, so distorted, so jolly, that the West would have to continue to wait for a more honest interpreter, for someone to balance that joyful release of emotion with that brooding "solitude, silence, and desolation" which Twain had seen and, for the time, rejected (thus, that special haunting quality inherent in the last lines of *Huckleberry Finn*, written when the freedom of the West had ended, written from the profound knowledge of the impossibility of escape: "I reckon

[48] Bernard DeVoto, ed., *Mark Twain in Eruption* (New York: Harper, 1940), p. 251.

I got to light out for the Territory"). But the West would wait in vain, for the myth of the heroic West is with Twain so firmly established and so widely disseminated that any other treatment will be henceforth reflected. The East seemed determined that the West should be romantic, and Twain concurred, and romantic therefore it was.

6

THE WESTERNERS:
Willa Cather

The wonder is in that barren land that she ever existed, and some kind of homage must be paid to her success, such as it was. The natives of Nebraska take well-warranted pride in their major cultural products: William Jennings Bryan, George Norris, the State Capitol building, and Willa Cather. They shaped the national scene in politics, social history, architecture, and literature, and the natives have to keep insisting on that in the face of a national tendency not to know even where Nebraska *is*. Willa Cather spoke of the New York critic who said, "I simply don't care a damn what happens in Nebraska, no matter who writes about it."[1] Defensive, unqualified praise is, however, wearisome and fruitless. Eventually one tires of panegyrics and notices that the Nebraska products are by any standard other than Nebraskan second-class, minor, joined by a common failure to carry the promise of greatness to fulfillment. There is a fault here

[1] Willa Cather, *On Writing* (New York: Knopf, 1949), p. 94.

which needs to be defined. Willa's case is classic, for she had
every conceivable gift: an inborn genius, a unique life in
a vital phase of history, the perfect education for writing, vig-
or of observation and depth of understanding, intellectual
maturity, a passionate devotion to craft — and then some flaw
defaced her every production such that even the most Nebraskan of critics is forced to qualify his praise. Her feminin-
ity is blamed: no mere *woman* can reach greatness; but this
is masculine snobbery. Her intellectual attitude is blamed:
an aristocrat, an anti-democrat, she could not possibly describe the American experience — as if Tolstoi could not delineate Russia from his position. Her search for values in the
past is blamed — as if Thoreau and Emerson were really for-
ward-looking, or Hemingway. Her literary structures are at-
tacked, ignoring her daring sense of form, her delicate experiments in tone; the haunting color of *Death Comes for the
Archbishop* or *The Professor's House* or *My Ántonia*, they
say, are based on demonstrably unclassic and ill-fitted assem-
blages of parts — as if she were not a contemporary of Crane
and Woolf and partner to them in impressionism. It is much
simpler to say that nothing great can by definition come from
Nebraska and let it go at that, except that further search will
uncover an even stranger explanation than any of these. It
involves Willa's movement from the West to the East, the
typical and necessary shaping that the East gives to the West
and the consequent flaw — here, in this case, reducible to its
origin in a mere room in Pittsburgh in 1901.

Her early life, as material for a nascent writer, was auspi-
cious. She was born, apparently, in 1873 — not, as she said,
in 1876[2] — near the village of Gore, deep in the ridge country of northwestern Virginia. The damp climate and the poor
land had made pioneers of her grandparents, who went west
in 1877; they were joined in 1883 by Willa's parents after a
barn and mill fire burned them out of Virginia. Willa's par-

[2] See the discussion by James R. Shively, ed., *Writings from Willa
Cather's Campus Years* (Lincoln: University of Nebraska Press, 1950),
pp. 14, 115–119.

ents lived with relatives on an overcrowded ranch northwest of Red Cloud, Nebraska, for a year and a half, and moved into a rented, overcrowded (there were seven children) house in Red Cloud in 1884. No farmer, Willa's father dealt in farm loans, abstracts, and insurance, comfortable enough in the then-thriving town.

But one must stop to realize what Red Cloud was like at that time. The frontier had swept on west, bypassing the Republican River valley so far from the main routes of travel. The valley itself was pleasant enough, but it was confined by high massive plains — treeless grassland, the two-thousand-mile-long and five-hundred-mile-wide Great Plains of the West. Furthermore, west of Lincoln an invisible boundary had to be crossed, the 100th meridian, west of which there would never be, consistently year after year, enough rainfall for feed crops. Settlers knew nothing of the boundary save what they learned by bitter experience, only preferring unconsciously the comfort of valleys with trees. And railroads tended to follow the valleys. Companies were formed to found towns in anticipation of the railroads, or the railroads themselves methodically laid out towns along their tracks (west of Lincoln are the alphabet towns of Crete, Dorchester, Exeter, Fairmont, Grafton, Harvard, etc.) inviting land development. Railroads and towns meant high land prices; thus it was the peasants, literally, who were driven up onto the open plains in search of cheap land — peasants direct from Germany, Sweden, Ireland, Bohemia, Russia, Austria, Norway, Poland. Red Cloud was established in 1870, the railroad came through in 1879, and Willa's parents in 1884. They came not to the frontier but to a settled and thriving community, not intellectual by any means, but polygot, with a society ranging from the future governor of the state (formed from the railroad aristocracy described in *A Lost Lady*) to the illiterate Bohemians (*My Ántonia*) who plowed land up "on the Divide," the prairies between the Republican River and the Blue. Yet they were predoomed, over half of them, to failure for having crossed the invisible line. Bitter cold, scorch-

ing heat, and wind without rain — these geographic facts unconsciously shaped and twisted the lives of the people. To
have been there at that time, to have seen the settlers of that
land, must have been one of the most beautiful moments of
our history; but it was also tragic. The dried lawns in Red
Cloud today, the boarded-up opera house, the turkey feath-
ers in the pit of the railroad roundhouse, these are the remains
of the history through which Willa Cather moved, for the
circle of history was completed in one lifetime; promise and
failure balanced each other like halves of a sphere; they are
called today romance and reality.

Only a young girl not tied to housework or to farm labor as
boys were could have roamed that country so freely. Perhaps
only a girl could have been sensitive to such virginal beauty
in the land. But it would have been meaningless to her without the base of comparison — the vaguely remembered life
of Virginia from which she had been so reluctantly torn —
and she was quick to see the inherent harshness of the condition of the new life, and just as quick to study the best
way to leave. We forget in this emancipated age the age-old
lack of freedom for women. How could she conceivably escape? What must it have been like to read Shakespeare in
that frigid attic room and listen at night to the whistle of a
train?

She developed a mania for education and for manhood. In
1888 she said she admired passion and nerve.[3] She dressed
as a boy and declared herself a doctor. The later mannish quality of Willa Cather which so concerned her contemporaries
and her later critics stems from this fifteen-year-old envy of
the freedom of choice of young boys, as well as her perfectly
normal love of her father and her brothers. She was called
"Willie." Her college associates were startled: "she was the
first girl that I ever saw in 'suspenders,'" remembered one of
them.[4] She wore suits and neckties and bobbed her hair. It

[3] Mildred R. Bennett, *The World of Willa Cather* (New York: Dodd,
Mead, 1951), p. 113.
[4] Shively, p. 124.

was part of her rebellion against the limitations of her sex, and it is echoed in her middy blouses, which she wore in competition with men in the masculine world of newspapers, and possibly in her later refusal to marry — lest she lose her hard-earned independence. In retrospect, she saw herself as a boy and narrated *My Ántonia, One of Ours,* and *A Lost Lady* from the points of view of sensitive youths. In maturity she was maternal, or, more precisely, maternally solicitous in the way of the maiden aunt which she was. Like other independent women of the day, she moved in the company of other independent women: Isabel McClung, Elizabeth Singer Sargent, and Edith Lewis; this was safe and proper to the life of the female artist in the 1900's. Perhaps she gained a sexual insight with her early-formulated attitude; perhaps she became aloof to the passions about which she wrote. At any rate, 1888 was when it began, when she professed to admire "amputating limbs" and "sliceing [*sic*] toads."[5] More important, with her masculine nerve she sat seriously to tutors in the town, reading Latin with William Drucker, listening to the French and German of Mrs. Charles Wiener, and she firmly demanded that she be allowed to go to the university at Lincoln. If she ever really intended to become a doctor, it must have been simply to get away — the same excuse Joyce used to get to Paris, simply to get away.

Thus began the first stage in her backward, fatal journey east. Geographically, she went only a hundred miles, but the world which opened up to her was so boundless that she could never again go back to stay in Red Cloud. To Lincoln, then, a lively prairie city with cultural aspirations, with opera and drama as weekly fare. It took her a year of pre-university work to satisfy the entrance requirements, and then there were four years of study in English, Greek, Latin, French, and German, with every day an invitation to more days and depths beyond.

Suddenly, on March 1, 1891, Willa appeared in print. A

[5] Bennett, pp. 112–113.

class essay on Carlyle was submitted by her English professor to the *Nebraska State Journal* and published with editorial praise. Overnight, as she said later, she changed from
a doctor into a writer.[6] No doubt her friendship with a class-
mate, Mariel Gere, influenced the editor of the paper, Charles
H. Gere, but a sharpened ability was certainly self-evident
by the time she ran a weekly column in the newspaper from
November, 1893, on; this, plus drama criticism at the rate of
$1 a night. At the university she plunged simultaneously into
student publications, becoming associate editor of the monthly *Lasso*, literary and then managing editor of the fortnightly
Hesperian, and editor of the annual, *The Sombrero*. Of course
she published some of her own stories. Most of these were
hardly worth reading, to say nothing of their republica-
tion in 1950.[7] With tolerant amusement we read the first
lines, "I, Kakau, son of Ramenka, high priest of Phtahah
in the great temple at Memphis, write this," or "Most of the
world knew him only as Yung Le Ho," or a satire, "Quick,
Gladys, get the other Gamma Gamma Lambda girls." Then
one's eye is caught by a line — "the brown, windswept prairies that never lead anywhere, but always stretch on and on
in a great yearning for something they never reach" — and
we are stirred. This in 1893 from a nineteen-year-old girl!
One reads further in disbelief. Here is a story of suicidal despair over the emptiness of "sun, and grass, and sky," ending
with the dead Anton frozen fast in a pool of his own blood.
Here is the Dane Lou, driven mad and mystic because he
had "stared into a black plow furrow all his life." Here is the
Russian Serge, who, with a hatchet, "clove through the man's
skull from crown to chin, even as the man had struck the

[6] *Ibid.*, p. 181.

[7] The stories quoted are in Shively, but this book has been super-
seded by a definitive collection: Willa Cather, *Collected Short Fiction,
1892–1912* (Lincoln: University of Nebraska Press, 1965). The first
discussion of the difference between Cather's early stories and her
later work is by Curtis Bradford, "Willa Cather's Uncollected Short
Stories," *American Literature*, XXVI (January, 1955), 537–551.

dog." They are melodramatic stories to be sure, wooden and ridiculous, rather like "sliceing toads," the bravado of a maverick female, but the recurring violence is tied so closely to the dreadful monotone of the Plains — this writing out of a revealing experience at the age of nineteen is enough to excuse the immaturity of the writing and to predict for the young Willa a boundless future.

Quite early she realized how far she had to go. Her high standards were set in an accidental meeting with Stephen Crane in 1894. It may not be quite as significant in literary history as that picnic meeting of Melville and Hawthorne, but it has its own overtones. Crane was on his way west and south, on his way to Mexico as a newspaper correspondent, to a year which produced nothing more than "The Blue Hotel," that formal tale of Crane's fatality rearranged in a Nebraska setting. Willa was on her way east. They met in the office of the *Journal* — and I prefer the legendary version that Crane was attracted to this girl because she was sound asleep standing up.[8] Willa's version may be more accurate:

The night was oppressively warm; one of those dry winds that are the curse of that country was blowing up from Kansas. The white, western moonlight threw sharp, blue shadows below us. The streets were silent at that hour, and we could hear the gurgle of the fountain in the Post Office square across the street, and the twang of banjos from the lower veranda of the Hotel Lincoln, where the colored waiters were serenading the guests. The drop lights in the office were dull in their green shades, and the telegraph sounder clicked faintly in the next room.[9]

The point is that Crane talked to her about the act of writing and about the bitter life of a writer and he set the poor girl on fire. The wonder is, even in 1900 when she wrote about it, that she should be so acutely aware of and sympathetic to the quality of his writing in spite of the shabbiness of the

[8] Edith Lewis, *Willa Cather Living, a Personal Record* (New York: Knopf, 1953), p. 37.
[9] Willa Cather, "When I Knew Stephen Crane," *The Library*, June 23, 1900, reprinted in *Prairie Schooner*, XXIII (Fall, 1949), 234.

actual man and her genteel notions of what a writer should be; but she had been well trained, even then. *The Red Badge of Courage* had been syndicated in the *Journal*, and it was Willa who had been called in to edit the faulty grammar of the copy. Yet at that age she could see beyond grammar. That crossing of two lives — he was twenty-four, she was twenty-one — has a night quality and the mournful memory of train whistles.

That was in her senior year, the same spring that she went to Chicago for the first time and saw opera every night for a week, the spring that she became an associate editor of a Lincoln society weekly, *The Courier*, edited by a Sarah Harris. She graduated — to no job, no future. Apparently her scorn for the mechanical critical technique of the English department head prevented her from being approved for a teaching job, her most obvious career, and though she continued in Lincoln and on the *Courier* until November, 1895, there was nothing for it but to go back home.

She must have written that year the story which was published in a national magazine in January, 1896, "On the Divide." The brutal Norwegian Canute in his loneliness seizes a neighborhood girl, forces a preacher to marry them, and then waits for the prairie loneliness to frighten her so she will accept him. Crane could have written such a sentence as this: "It causes no great sensation there when a Dane is found swinging to his own windmill tower, and most of the Poles after they have become too careless and discouraged to shave themselves keep their razors to cut their throats with." [10] Crane would have admired the symbols inherent in the rattlesnake skins and in Canute's wood carvings — "It was a veritable Dance of Death by one who had felt its sting" — and the rhythm and the mood of a passage such as this:

He knew by heart every individual clump of bunchgrass in the miles of red shaggy prairie that stretched before his cabin. He

[10] Willa Cather, *Early Stories*, Mildred R. Bennett, ed. (New York: Dodd, Mead, 1957), p. 63.

knew it in all the deceitful loveliness of its early summer, in all the bitter barrenness of its autumn. He had seen it smitten by all the plagues of Egypt. He had seen it parched by drought, and sogged by rain, beaten by hail, and swept by fire, and in the grasshopper years he had seen it eaten as bare and clean as bones that the vultures have left. After the great fires he had seen it stretch for miles and miles, black and smoking as the floor of hell.[11]

This is Naturalism at its best, but that is a word never applied to the later work of Willa Cather.

She was rescued by the Gere family, who introduced her to George Axtell, who promptly hired her as an editor of a new magazine, *The Home Monthly*, to be published in Pittsburgh. The Red Cloud *Chief* of June 26, 1896, recorded her departure on the second stage of her journey east.

The next ten years of her life present some confusion unless we arrange them in order of her various occupations. Willa Cather was an editor of *The Home Monthly* for only one year, though she sent contributions to the magazine for two more years, through December, 1899.[12] Her next work was with the Pittsburgh *Leader* as assistant to the telegraph editor and as one of several reviewers of theater, opera, and books. This work extended from September, 1897, through March, 1900 (in the same period she also sent newspaper copy back to the Lincoln *Journal* and *Courier*). A third employment was as a free-lance contributor to another new and short-lived literary magazine, *The Library*, extending from April to December, 1900. The fourth was as a Latin teacher in the Central High School for the spring term, 1901, and as English teacher in that school and at the Alleghany High School from the fall of 1901 until her departure for New York and *McClure's* in the summer of 1906. Thus she was editor, reporter, critic, and free-lance contributor for about five years and high school teacher for a second five years, the dividing line being March, 1901.

[11] *Ibid.*, p. 61.
[12] Details of this period in Miss Cather's career are most fully reported in John P. Hinz, "Willa Cather in Pittsburgh," *The New Colophon, III* (New York, 1950), 198–207.

In spite of this arrangement, a writer's growth cannot be plotted on a straight-line graph. Although, in retrospect, we can see an ultimate accomplishment and thus label this or that as false direction, away from the true line of the graph, a truer graph is of consecutive or overlapping lines, one beginning before another ends, and some lines partly on and partly off the true, but the sum stabilizing or fixed in direction after a certain point has been reached. If we could have plotted the ideal writer from the base of Willa Cather's birth, we would find no major fault with the general line taken thus far—up to about 1901. Willa had to go on to the East, to a maturity in thought and motive. The possible directions she could go had begun to narrow down; but her development was still more or less fluid. Nor could one complain about the forthcoming career in journalism and hack-writing. The knowledge of words grows with use and with the growing experience in the world; and the timeless prairie would wait for her return.

She lived in a boarding house, with a screen separating her desk from her bed. She bicycled to work or rode the streetcar. She had to find writers for this new magazine, a pale imitation of the *Ladies' Home Journal*, or write *The Home Monthly* herself. She bought what she could and began an editor's masquerade: Sibert, Henry Nicklemann, Helen Delay, John Charles Asten, John Esten, Mary Temple Bayard, Mary Temple Jamison, Clara Wood Shipman, C. W. S., George Overing, W. Bert Foster, Gilberta S. Whittle—these were all Willa Cather.[13] These people wrote, for the most part, trash. But Willa was alive, working, independent, and happy. She stopped regularly at the home of a contributor, George Seibel, who held solo "French soirees" for Willa. They read together Daudet, de Musset, France, Gautier, Hugo, Verlaine, Baudelaire, and Flaubert.[14] Willa moved on to the *Leader*, where, as a book reviewer, she was astute and modern enough to

[13] *Ibid.*, pp. 200–203.
[14] George Seibel, "Miss Willa Cather from Nebraska," *The New Colophon*, II (New York, 1949), 198.

praise *McTeague* and damn *The Gentleman from Indiana*.
She continued the drama reviews begun in Lincoln and even
made up the manuscript of a first book, *The Player Letters*,
by 1899, though she was unable to find a publisher for it.[15]
She wrote doggerel verse and sketches of all sorts. As editor
of *The Home Monthly* she published her own stories and sent
others to national magazines. Some of these were very bad.
"The Count of Crow's Nest" in 1896 told of the destitute
Count de Koch's efforts to protect his family papers from
his avaricious daughter. Some were amusing. "The Affair at
Gover's Station" was a railroad murder-and-ghost tale. Others were good. "Eric Hermannson's Soul," in *Cosmopolitan*,
1900, tells of a rigid prairie Free Gospeller who gladly sells his
soul to kiss a beautiful girl from the East — this on a ladder
of a windmill tower: Faust in a new setting. The sum, however, is shabby imitation of Paul Leicester Ford or very bad
Henry James. These were all false directions, yet part of a
necessary apprenticeship.

Then, in March, 1901, the entire direction of the line on
the graph shifted: Willa met rich, handsome Isabel McClung
in the theater dressing room of the actress Lizzie Hudson Collier. Isabel was in revolt against the Scotch Presbyterian rigid-
ity of her father, a conservative and eminent judge. She had
adopted Art as her weapon and sought out writers, painters,
musicians, and actors — anyone foreign, non-Pittsburgh. She
was a patroness of the arts and she seized on Willa and moved
her into the McClung mansion for five years. It is easy enough
to understand Isabel's part in this act, but more difficult to
understand Willa's. The women who knew her best describe
it thus: "Willa had more natural affinity for *la vie de famille*
than for *la vie de boheme*: after her long bout with uncon-
genial surroundings she enjoyed the protected, delicately
nurtured life of the well-to-do";[16] and "she enjoyed a tran-

[15] F. B. Adams, Jr., "Willa Cather's Early Years: Trial and Error,"
Colophon, New Graphic Series, I (New York, 1939), 92.
[16] Elizabeth Shepley Sergeant, *Willa Cather, a Memoir* (Philadelphia: Lippincott, 1953), p. 20.

quillity and physical comfort in the McClung house she had probably never before experienced." [17] The women shared a bedroom. A sewing room was fitted out as a study for Willa. Then Judge McClung arranged for Willa's teaching job and, no doubt, financed the trip to Europe of Willa and Isabel in 1902 (and, I suspect, the publication of *April Twilights* in 1903). The relationship was one of feminine companionship, but under these happy auspices Willa Cather's writing began to change.

She continued her hack-writing, chiefly in the Pittsburgh *Gazette*, but in a lesser quantity than before 1901. She published several short stories, some of which were to appear in book form in *The Troll Garden*, 1905. She also published the volume of twenty-seven poems called *April Twilights*, 1903, through a vanity publisher, Richard G. Badger, Gorham Press, who accompanied the slim volume with a spectacular review in *Poet Lore* (owned by the Gorham Press).[18] If the book served to get classical-pastoral poetry out of her system, the book served well; if it taught Willa that her forte was a rhythmic prose and not formal poetry, it taught well indeed. The rest can be dismissed. The poems are derivative and lifeless. They are based on classical reading or on her recent enthusiasm for Housman ("Shepherd lads with silver hair, / Shepherd maids no longer fair"). Anything close to Willa's own experience from which a vitality might come easily is ornamented with extraneous references. "White Birch in Wyoming" dwells on Burne-Jones and Brunhilda. "The Night Express" goes by way of Shropshire: "To earth I digged in boyhood, through fields I used to keep, / The lads who wrought beside me shall bear me home to sleep." The emphasis is on London and Paris, a direct result of the 1902 trip with Isabel.

Willa had reported on the trip, supposedly to help pay ex-

[17] Lewis, p. 54.

[18] Willa Cather, *April Twilights*, Bernice Slote, ed. (Lincoln: University of Nebraska Press, 1962), p. xix. Further quotations from this text are not footnoted.

penses, fourteen articles to the *Nebraska State Journal.* The
new European orientation is evident in her enthusiasm and
in her careful reportorial eye: the pilgrimage to Housman,
the studio of Burne-Jones, the Barbizon country of Millet and
Rousseau, the Papal Palace at Avignon, and a fishing village
on the Mediterranean, Le Lavandau. Their only interest for
us is in, to quote the editor of a recent edition of the articles,
"her first experiences amid all the heaped-up riches, the accumulated treasure, of European civilization, feeling deeply
its weight and glory, its past and present." [19] The writing is
mature enough, but unexceptional. A change of values is evident in every line: "The dinner consisted of ten courses, each
better than the last, with wines that made us sad because we
knew we would never taste their like again. Little white fish,
just caught in the Rhone and popped into the pan, calf's head
with tomato sauce, lamp chops with a wonderful sauce of
spinach, big yellow melons and figs and grapes, cream of car-
rot soup and patties of rice, broiled larks on toast, and marvelous little cakes made of honey and spice and flour." Thus
was fulfilled her decade of reading French literature. Rarely
does she attempt to bridge the two worlds. "The long even
stretch of yellow stubble, broken here and there by a pile of
Lombard poplars, recalled not a little the country about
Campbell and Bladen [Nebraska], and is certainly more familiar than anything I have seen of this side of the Atlantic."
She finds an American-made reaper and recalls her own delight in riding along on one. She admires the "brown, merry
old women" and finds them with their "blithe songs" and
"good-humoured remarks" exactly like the paintings of Millet. She was not homesick when she wrote that, or very realistic. The influence of Crane was past. Willa had begun to paint
pretty pictures with words.

In such company and, back in Pittsburgh, from such a house,
what else could she have written besides *April Twilights?*
There are four stories published in the 1901-06 period which

[19] George N. Kates, ed., *Willa Cather in Europe* (New York: Knopf,
1956), p. vii. Further quotations from this text are not footnoted.

have a Western background, and they reveal the increasingly narrow range of scope still available to Willa Cather. They range from poor writing to her best writing yet.

The first of these, "El Dorado: A Kansas Recessional," published in the *New England Magazine*, June, 1901, has the mark of the harshly realistic writing we have seen in earlier writing. A western Kansas land swindle is described, the Gump family luring Virginians to the West and then absconding with funds, leaving behind one Josiah Bywaters, sole resident of the desolate town. The story begins with a familiar Cather scene: "Across the river stretched the level land like the top of an oven. It was a country flat and featureless, without tones or shadows, without accent or emphasis of any kind to break its vast monotony. It was a scene done entirely in high lights, without relief, without a single commanding eminence to rest the eye upon. The flat plains rolled to the unbroken horizon vacant and void, forever reaching in empty yearning toward something never attained." [20] The last sentence is a near copy of a sentence previously quoted from a story written in 1893. But the story ends in sheer vapid romance: Apollo Gump returns to retrieve mementoes of his marriage to an actress, is bitten by a rattlesnake and dies, and Josiah Bywaters escapes the empty town with Apollo's money. The story uses the Western setting only for hack work.

The second is vastly different. "The Treasure of Far Island," October, 1902, records the happy return of a successful playwright to Empire City, Nebraska, on the Republican River (Willa's daydreams are obvious), where he proposes to his childhood sweetheart. The descriptions are idyllic as the two adults return to a sandbar and dig up the treasure they buried in their childhood. They recall their pirate fantasies:

"It is strange how those wild imaginings of ours seem, in retrospect, realities, things that I actually lived through. I suppose that in cold fact my life was a good deal like that of other little girls who grow

[20] Willa Cather, "El Dorado: A Kansas Recessional," *New England Magazine*, N.S., XXIV (June, 1901), 357.

up in a village; but whenever I look back on it, it is all exultation and romance, — sea fights and splendid galleys and Roman triumphs and brilliant caravans winding through the desert."

"To people who live by imagination at all, that is the only life that goes deep enough to leave memories." [21]

The statement is revealing of the creative process, how a physical environment becomes transformed by memory. However, the stilted conversation and the superficial characters make the story another example of hack work, hardly relevant to the Nebraska setting.

The third story is "'A Death in the Desert,'" 1903, a story of a concert singer's love for a composer, recalled by the woman in Wyoming dying of consumption. The Western setting is of trifling concern, except where the stolid husband of the singer retraces her life: "'She was a great woman, as you say, and she didn't come of a great family. She had to fight her own way from the first. She got to Chicago, and then to New York, and then to Europe, where she went up like lightning, and got a taste for it all; and now she's dying here like a rat in a hole, out of her own world, and she can't fall back into ours.'" [22] The grand passion, described in its setting of an "old palace" in Florence, makes the story dull indeed. The author is romanticizing, putting into print another daydream which contrasts vividly with the "desert" of the West, and feeling sorry for herself.

The next three stories, republished in *The Troll Garden*, are of a different quality; they are among the best Willa Cather ever wrote, and we must generously credit Isabel McClung with providing the opportunity for such mature creation as they represent. Each story is a model of its kind, but our concern here is the use of a Western setting. Is there a "wrong" or a "right" tone to take? For the moment all we can do is describe the tone as a definite change from the ear-

[21] Willa Cather, "The Treasure of Far Island," *New England Magazine*, N.S., XXVII (October, 1902), 247.

[22] Willa Cather, *The Troll Garden* (New York: McClure, Phillips, 1905), p. 121. Further quotations from this text are not footnoted.

lier writing. These three stories mark clearly the assumption of new values.

"A Wagner Matinee," 1904, is a rather poignant tale of a New England music teacher whose marriage exiled her to the Nebraska frontier for thirty years; returning to a Boston concert, an old and withered woman, her heart is re-awakened by Wagner's music, and she pleads not to have to go back to Nebraska, to the "inconceivable silence of the plains." The narrator is the woman's nephew Clark, a bachelor living in Boston but brought up in Nebraska, educated by his Aunt Georgiana. He is Willa Cather's now-familiar masculine disguise and we can assume Clark's statements are Willa's. A fastidious contrast is drawn between Nebraska — "the tall, unpainted house, with weather-curled boards" — and the East as represented by the orchestra — "the restless, wind-tossed forest of fiddle necks and bows." The music is the "power which had kindled the world" and Aunt Georgiana's work-worn hands express the thirty-year drought of her soul. The Nebraska frontier was "waste and wear" and a renunciation of all hope, in contrast to the fulfillment of culture. There is no bridging of the gulf, and East is held to be far superior to West.

More viciously, the same contrast is drawn in "The Sculptor's Funeral," 1905. The coffin of a world-renowned sculptor, Harvey Merrick, is returned to his Kansas home town for burial. The event is described by one of the sculptor's pupils, who accompanies the coffin to the Merrick family home, and by Jim Laird, a drunken lawyer who assails the meanness of the people of the town because they cannot appreciate the sculptor's worth. Thus, Willa Cather is in three guises: the artist, the fastidious Easterner, and the man who assails the West. The "desert of newness and ugliness and sordidness" is contrasted with "all that is chastened and old, and noble with traditions." The "bitter, dead little Western town," the "hog wallow," the "dung heap," though the source of genius, is in all its aspects held in disdain. Such terms as these in 1905 anticipate the later national Revolt from the Village which preoccupied so many writers in the Twenties. Here it is the rural-urban strife overlaid with East-West conflict — the New World and the Old, with the Old World, of course, the better. The bitterness in this Cather story is clearly different from either the earlier realistic work on Nebraska or the later idyllic versions in *O Pioneers!* and *My Ántonia.* "The Sculptor's Funeral" is a powerful little story, but it is not in a mood one can sustain over a lifetime. As Miss Cather said, "Nearly all very young authors write sad stories in revolt against everything. Humor, kindliness, tolerance come late." [23]

The last important short story of the period, though not Western in its setting, is the most significant of all: "Paul's Case," 1905. An unusual high school student exasperates his teachers with his contemptuous attitude, which Willa Cather then traces to its source: the contrast he feels between his mean life in an ugly row of houses in Pittsburgh and the art he has discovered in galleries, concert halls, and theaters. When these releases are stopped for him (his father forces him to quit his job as an usher and take a clerk's job), he steals money, goes to New York, and lives at the Waldorf until his money runs out, and then in the end kills himself. The story is uneven: the Paul at the end is different from the Paul at the beginning. It is also evident that Willa herself was uncertain what tone to take, and the story ends in a Wertherian melodrama (the same violence ends the forthcoming novels, *Alexander's Bridge* and *O Pioneers!*). The narrator of the story is the omniscient author — not a disinterested psychoanalyst but a person extremely sympathetic to Paul's case, which somehow represents in symbolic fashion Willa's own case at this time. She, too, came from a mean background, or, more precisely, one which seemed mean in contrast to what wealth could attain. "After each of these orgies of living in the theater he experienced all the physical depression which follows a debauch; the loathing of respectable beds, of common food, of a house penetrated by kitchen odors; a shud-

[23] Quoted by Bennett, *The World of Willa Cather,* p. 199.

dering repulsion for the flavorless, colorless mass of every-
day existence; a morbid desire for cool things and soft lights
and fresh flowers." Perhaps this is Willa describing her boarding house in Pittsburgh and explaining why she moved to the
McClung mansion. Paul had fallen in love with Romance.
When he enters the dressing room of a juvenile actor friend
(I suppose there is no anagram in naming him Charley Edwards, though Willa's friend had been Lizzie or Elizabeth Collier), he "felt within him the possibility of doing or
saying splendid, brilliant, poetic things." "Perhaps it was because, in Paul's world, the natural nearly always wore the
guise of ugliness, that a certain element of artificiality seemed
to him necessary in beauty." This sounds very much like Willa
saying that the artifice of art is necessary to sustain one in
this ugly world. But Paul goes on to New York, to the pleasures of flowers in winter, clean linen, "the roseate tinge of his
champagne," and a little sadly admits that money stood between the two worlds: "money was everything, the wall that
stood between all he loathed and all he wanted." Willa,
of course, did not want only the mere sensual pleasures of
Paul's extravagances and she did not kill herself once she had
tasted delight. But the tone of the story seems to say in a sad
self-knowledge: I will operate from this base — of culture and
wealth. If this interpretation seems to be pushing autobiography too far, anticipate the drive of Mrs. Forrester of *A Lost
Lady* to leave her little Nebraska town at whatever cost; or
realize again how far from Red Cloud Willa Cather had to go
in order to write such a tale as this.

These tales matter not at all unless they have predicted
or predetermined a certain failure in her later career, now
more and more restricted in direction as she moved on east.

When Willa Cather was thirty-one, the publisher of *The
Troll Garden* collection went to Pittsburgh to inspect his new
author and ended his stay with Judge McClung by hiring
Willa as an associate editor of *McClure's Magazine*. Willa left
Pittsburgh in the summer of 1906 and worked for S. S. Mc-
Clure until autumn, 1911, when she began writing "The Bohe-

mian Girl," the story which evolved into *O Pioneers!* (1913).

The McClure period is distinguished by the publication of a handful of short stories (unimpressive except for "The Enchanted Bluff"), and the first novel, *Alexander's Bridge*, 1912. She also worked as an editor of S. S. McClure's *Autobiography* and on Georgine Milmine's *Mary Baker G. Eddy: The Story of Her Life and History of Christian Science*. Her work was like her early Pittsburgh magazine work, only on a larger scale. Her residences were once again inconvenient and drab—a studio building on Washington Square and a French hotel on Ninth Street—but enhanced by the beauty of Old New York and a neighborhood of Bohemia (in 1909 she moved with Edith Lewis, a *McClure's* writer, to an apartment on Washington Place and in 1912 to her permanent residence at 5 Bank Street). What is different is the national (and international, for McClure sent her to England in 1909) scale of her activities. Especially important was the trip to Boston in 1908 to work over the Christian Science material.

There, through a friendship with Mrs. Louis Brandeis, she met Mrs. Fields, the widow of Hawthorne's publisher, and the local-color writer, Sarah Orne Jewett. The significance of all this is made clear in Miss Cather's essay: "The unique charm of Mrs. Fields' house was not that it was a place where one could hear about the past, but that it was a place where the past lived on—where it was protected and cherished, had sanctuary from the noisy push of the present."[24] And it is significant too in the admiration Willa felt for Miss Jewett, both for her personality—"a lady, in the high old sense . . . an ease, a graciousness"—and for her prose. When Willa defines in 1925 the ultimate quality of imaginative literature for Miss Jewett—"One might say that every fine story must leave in the mind of the sensitive reader an intangible residuum of pleasure; a cadence, a quality of voice that is exclusively the writer's own, individual, unique"—she is explaining the qualities of prose which she herself adopted by

[24] Willa Cather, *Not Under Forty* (New York: Knopf, 1936), p. 61. Further quotations from this text are not footnoted.

way of Boston. She learned from Miss Jewett where her own genius lay. "A reporter can write equally well about everything that is presented to his view, but a creative writer can do his best only with what lies within the range and character of his deepest sympathies." She learned that she had to go back to Nebraska for her subjects. But the route was to be devious, and ultimately she did not arrive at Nebraska at all.

First, she had to write that Bostonian, London, Jamesian drawing-room drama called *Alexander's Bridge*, named after the bridge-building hero who had conquered a world. The excessive passion of Bartley Alexander, caught between the love for his elegant Boston wife and the love for a vivacious London actress, destroys him. The novel is clearly a product of an Eastern point of view. Miss Cather describes its source: "My first novel, *Alexander's Bridge*, was very like what painters call a studio picture. It was the result of meeting some interesting people in London. Like most young writers, I thought a book should be made out of 'interesting material,' and at that time I found the new more exciting than the familiar. The impressions I tried to communicate on paper were genuine, but they were shallow." [25] It seems an honest self-criticism. After this book, she speaks of recovering from the "conventional editorial point of view" on her first trip to Arizona and New Mexico in the summer of 1911 and then making the crucial change. "When I got back to Pittsburgh [and from Pittsburgh on to Cherry Valley, New York, where she took a house with Isabel McClung] I began to write a book entirely for myself . . . [about] a kind of country I loved." [26] This was to be *O Pioneers!*

The education of the writer is completed, the true line on the graph is found, and the culmination of experience, standards, and ability should have produced a masterpiece. It didn't. The failings of *O Pioneers!* are the failings of the later novels; they must be spelled out.

[25] Cather, *On Writing*, p. 91.
[26] *Ibid.*, pp. 92–93.

O Pioneers! is a strangely disjointed work, apparently assembled from disparate elements and story fragments written
previous to the concept of the novel.[27] In Part One, "The
Wild Land," the Bergson family is presented: the dying immigrant father; the bewildered and useless mother;
two oxen-like sons, Lou and Oscar; a younger sensitive son,
Emil; and Alexandra, fresh and lovely in her early twenties,
the strong one of the family who guides them through the
lean years of drought. Part Two, "Neighboring Fields," resumes the family chronicle sixteen years later. Lou and Oscar
have married and own farms of their own. Alexandra runs the
family home; she is single, but attracted to a former neighbor, Carl Linstrom, now returned for a visit. But the emphasis is on Emil, now a university student and falling in love
with Marie Shabata, the pretty wife of another neighbor.
Part Three, "Winter Memories," is a short passage marking
the absence of both Carl and Emil. Part Four, "The White
Mulberry Tree," describes the events leading to the murder
of Emil and Marie by Frank Shabata. Part Five, "Alexandra,"
summarizes: Alexandra visits Frank at the penitentiary, for-
gives him, and returns home to accept marriage to Carl. Thus,
the plot devolves on the affair of Emil and Marie — the whirl-
ing motion of passion around the unmoved Alexandra, a passive observer from the beginning of Part Two on. Alexandra
came from "The Bohemian Girl" and she is also the feminine
of Alexander in the previous novel, whose bridge-building
dominated a world; Alexander's destructive passion is here
transferred to Marie and Emil. Instead of one story, there are
two: the character sketch of Alexandra, which overlaps or is
succeeded by the passion of Emil and Marie — and the latter
tale consumes more than half of the total. Clearly, however,
the sympathies of the author are with the surviving Alexandra, not with the passion, even though Alexandra herself is
presented woodenly and not in the depth or detail with which
Emil and Marie are described.

[27] E. K. Brown, *Willa Cather, a Critical Biography* (New York:
Knopf, 1953), p. 173.

The novel is laced together with seemingly extraneous material which can best be described as local-color sketches: Crazy Ivar, the French fair, the confirmation service, the life and death of Amedee Chevalier. Each chapter, in fact, is presented as a separate sketch, a kind of tone poem, on figures in a landscape. For example, Part Two begins with a beautiful and foreboding scene: Emil is cutting the long grass in the Norwegian graveyard and Marie stops by in a horse-cart, a lovely moment of shared rhythms. This episodic technique is intended to give the "intangible residuum of pleasure" mentioned previously, as the reader reflects on each scene. The seemingly disparate elements are held together by the figure of Alexandra, if she is seen as the critic Daiches sees her, "as a kind of Earth Mother or Corn Goddess, a Ceres who presides over the fruitful land, symbol of the success of the pioneers in taming the reluctant but immensely promising soil."[28]

Alexandra is passive and receptive. Once she has held the family together in the lean years (to page 71), she is helpless and immobile, indeed completely blind to the dangerous affair of Emil and Marie, unimaginative and unable to recognize evil in anything. She concludes the novel with an oracular and placid vision, completely out of character: "We come and go, but the land is always here. And the people who love it and understand it are the people who own it — for a little while."[29] We suspect the judgment as Willa's, but we look for her first in the young male characters. She is young Emil at the university at Lincoln with his love of music (he plays a cornet) and his restless winter in a foreign country (Mexico) and in his plans to go farther east (to Ann Arbor). She is also in Carl Linstrom with his early departure from Nebraska and his love of art and his trips back to Nebraska to interpret to Alexandra the significance of the fam-

[28] David Daiches, *Willa Cather, a Critical Introduction* (Ithaca, New York: Cornell University Press, 1951), p. 28.
[29] Willa Cather, *O Pioneers!* (Boston: Houghton Mifflin, 1913), p. 308. Further quotations from this text are not footnoted.

ily history, as he does in the last chapter. But Willa is superior
to the passion of Emil and to the woodenness of Carl; she is
Alexandra herself, statuesque and above the others: "'I
think when friends marry, they are safe. We don't suffer
like — those young ones,' Alexandra ended with a sigh." To
me, there is something terribly patronizing about that. The
"quality of voice" here is idolizing, exterior, and benign.

It is, I am afraid, a novel written by an outsider, a dispas-
sionate peopling of Nebraska with the peasants of Millet.
What the novel is not is immediately clear if we recall the previous Nebraska characters with which she began her writing
career: the suicide Peter Sadelack, the prophet Lou, the
murderer Serge Dovolitchly, the lecherous Canute, and the
damned Eric Hermannson; then the town swine in "The
Sculptor's Funeral" and the pathetic Aunt Georgiana of "A
Wagner Matinee" — these lively people are reduced to the
pleasantness of Crazy Ivar and the explained-away murders
by Frank Shabata. Moreover, the storms, blights, droughts,
fires, blizzards, plagues of the earlier stories have all but disappeared. The first line of the book — "One January day, thirty years ago, the little town of Hanover, anchored on a windy
Nebraska tableland, was trying not to be blown away" — indicates a pleasant, mild attitude to the ruthless ferocity of a
Nebraska ground blizzard.

What Willa Cather had now chosen to write about is made
startlingly clear by comparison with the work of another Nebraskan, Mari Sandoz. Her country in *Old Jules* is two hundred miles north of Red Cloud, though not a very different
setting. Miss Sandoz chooses another emphasis. "The drouth
exceeded all probability. Corn did not sprout. On the hard-
land fringe the buffalo grass was started and browned before the first of May. Even lighter soil south of the river
produced nothing." [30] "One window after another crashed in-
ward, the force of the wind blowing the blankets and sheets
into the room, driving the hail in spurts across the floor." "The

[30] Mari Sandoz, *Old Jules* (Boston: Little, Brown, 1935), p. 179.
Further quotations from this text are not footnoted.

whole damn sandhills is deserted. The cattlemen are broke, the settlers about gone. I got to start all over."

Willa Cather chose not to write about such things. I suggest that in an effort to please the McClungs and McClure and Mrs. Fields and Miss Jewett, she chose the rosy tints of romanticism, which inhibit all of her later writings about the West. She chose to write an idyll or a pastorale. Beautiful as it may be, it hasn't the strength or the vigor or the reality of the history itself. She has polished and tamed a land and its people out of all recognition. She did this, she had to do this in self-defense; who cared, after all, about Nebraska? She had come, by 1913, to write from the point of view of the East, substituting artifice for truth.

7

THE WESTERNERS:
Bernard DeVoto

But the frontier had "closed" in 1890. There were, there remained thousands of square miles of unoccupied land, but the telegraph poles, the railroads, and the small towns — and with them the law and institutions of the East — had created by 1890 a vastly different country, different, that is, from the West. Homogenizing processes all the way from traveling salesmen to United States senators would alter forever everything but the wind, the rock, and the sun. Utah, for example, would give up its own peculiar institution in order to sell copper. For a time there was a tension and an awareness and then, to use the term of California journalist Neil Morgan, there was a westward tilt: the Eastern population headed for the Western sea as in a marmot drive; Indians bought rugs manufactured in Massachusetts; the Union Pacific publicized dude ranches; and God created Hollywood to remind us of what had been lost.

There was (there is, possibly, still) an interim of change. We have waited all this time for a writer skilled enough and perceptive enough to write about the West without inherent distortion, to see man in relationship to a powerful and terrible nature (the canyon, the desert, the upsurge of mountains), but more to sing his freedom than to mourn his losses. But the moment such an awareness came, the change was so advanced that the terms could only be of retrospect and loss. Such is the moral, at any rate, of the short swift life of Bernard Augustine DeVoto bracketed by its meaningful dates, 1897-1955. Place of birth, Utah; of death, New York. From West to East.

He is the first bona fide native of the West we have studied — as if this might make a difference, for any person is a product of his ancestry more than his environment, a composite of his ancestry; any American is a product of the melting pot in which the European heritage is muddled but never quite lost. But DeVoto's case is an anomaly. His paternal grandfather was an Italian cavalry officer who immigrated to America, sired two children, died, and left his widow ill and helpless in Cairo, Illinois.[1] This Maria Antonia DeVoto gave her children as wards to one Mother Augusta of the Sisters of the Holy Cross at Notre Dame, Indiana; thus the orphaned son was able to receive a very fine education. In 1876 Florian DeVoto followed the missionary efforts of the Church to Salt Lake City and north of there thirty-six miles to Ogden. Florian made Ogden his home and became a railroad freight agent and an abstractor of titles, a studious man of modest means.

Bernard's maternal grandfather, Samuel Dye, was an Englishman and a convert to Mormonism who moved west at the outbreak of the Civil War and established a fruit farm at Uintah at the mouth of Ogden Canyon. One of his daughters,

---

[1] Biographical details are subject to closer study; DeVoto was not above exaggeration for effect. I summarize here without footnotes my own investigations in "The Work of Bernard DeVoto, Introduction and Annotated Check List," unpublished dissertation, State University of Iowa, 1957. See also Catherine Drinker Bowen *et al.*, *Four Portraits and One Subject: Bernard DeVoto* (Boston: Houghton Mifflin, 1963).

Rhoda, a divorcée with one son, married Florian and moved into town. Both Florian and Rhoda became church apostates; but the complex is there in the background, the authoritarian churches in a wild land.

The wild land was not so wild by the time Bernard was born in 1897. The Union Pacific trains debouched shrieking and echoing from the lips of the canyon and squealed around corners to the railroad yards in Ogden. The Wasatch Mountains descend abruptly to the great basin, and although the wilderness is never very far away, the plain is civilized by a series of towns perched on ledges between the mountains and the Salt Lake. Bernard's fiction plays with the contrast between the plains and the mountains; the two local canyons, the Ogden and the Weber, are the openings to freedom.

But there were more than normal restrictions. Some quirk of the parents kept Bernard in the Sacred Heart Academy after his male classmates had moved on to a parochial school; from the fifth through the eighth grades "Bernardo" was the only boy in a roomful of girls, thoroughly disliked but brilliant and a teacher's pet: "he was contentious, captious, critical, quick to scorn; he affected superiorities and was constantly in controversies and in his bad spells was desolated that some people didn't like him."[2] On top of this he was ugly; his body was short and stocky; his face was dominated by a misshapen nose: "his nostrils were like those of a man seen supine."[3] In addition he had to work: driving a delivery wagon, working as a baggage and ticket agent, assisting the Weber county clerk, reporting baseball games for the Ogden *Standard* — onerous chores only because Ogden had developed by the time of Bernard's high school years a social strata of the rich and idle, which acted as a gore. His restrictions became drives and energies.

To his basic intelligence and sensitivity and emotional complexity knowledge had to be added beyond the miscellany

[2] Wallace Stegner in *ibid.*, p. 91.

[3] A. B. Guthrie, Jr., *The Blue Hen's Chick* (New York: McGraw-Hill, 1964), p. 190.

of reading material available to him in Ogden through Spargo's Book Store or in his high school. He went first, in 1914, to the University of Utah at Salt Lake City (probably not through his own choice), attaching himself to the English instructors and publishing in the campus magazine his first short story. A university quarrel concerning supposed Mormon influence on curriculum led to the dismissal of the English instructors — and DeVoto had his excuse to go east.

Thus the transformation began. I use the phrase DeVoto himself used in speaking of Mark Twain: "He came East and he accepted tuition."[4] The argument here is that he could never have written about the West from the point of view only of the West. Some kind of perspective — literary or geographical — seems to be necessary to the writer to avoid provincialism and mere local color. The writer has to grow up; his learning must be fitted to some scheme beyond the confines of his home (even Thoreau is no exception to the rule), although the results of his education are yet another tension, described most briefly and easily by Thomas Wolfe's phrase, "You can't go home again."

He went to Harvard with a career in medicine in mind, probably in emulation of his first roommate, an Ogden man who became a doctor. But his literature teachers — Irving Babbitt, LeBaron Russell Briggs, Byron Satterlee Hurlbut, Charles Townsend Copeland — soon had him writing essays, poetry, and short stories. Nevertheless he worked alone, a barbarian without name or money. A contemporary, Malcolm Cowley, describes the new set of tensions:

Harvard in those days was cool to Western highschool boys, a fact that might help to explain DeVoto's magnification of the West at the expense of New York and New England, but Harvard was even cooler to undergraduates who had first attended other colleges; they missed the easier friendships of the freshman year and seldom played much part in student activities. DeVoto was eventually assigned to the class of 1918, but he must have remained an

---

[4] Bernard DeVoto, *Mark Twain's America* (Boston: Little, Brown, 1932), p. 207.

out-of-course student until he went off to the army; for neither his name nor his picture appears in the class album. He was outside the college social world of dinners, punches and Boston dances; that wouldn't have bothered him much. But he was also outside the college literary world, which was thriving in those days; it included Cummings and Dos Passos among others.[5]

DeVoto left Harvard when America entered the war; the Western sharpshooter became an instructor in marksmanship, going from one army camp to another, and returned to Harvard to graduate in June, 1920. He considered job offers on the New York *Sun* and the *New Republic* and then he did what Wolfe would say you can't do — he went home.

The death of his mother in 1919 may have influenced him; or he was ill from a bout of influenza; or he was in love — DeVoto himself could not recall why. "I don't know why in hell I went back to Ogden. There's something about that country that's hard to get away from."[6]

He stayed two nightmarish years. He clerked in Spargo's Book Store; he taught history in the Mound Fort Junior High School; he worked on a hay gang; he prospected for gold; he plunged into local and state politics by joining the local American Legion and by working as secretary of the Weber County Democratic Committee; he wrote one or two novels; he fell desperately in love with a beautiful woman — she spurned him (I have seen the letters which he wrote her, which she did not bother to read, which he came to know she had not read) and married the doctor he had roomed with at Harvard — and he suffered a nervous collapse. Late in the summer of 1922 he was hired by telegram to teach English at Northwestern University, and made permanent the move from West to East.

He was now like a mainspring wound tight, or like a strung arrow, aimed, ready for release. I believe his ambition and his direction were fixed in the years 1920-22 in the dis-

[5] Malcolm Cowley, "Marginalia," *The New Republic*, CX (April 17, 1944), 537.

[6] Bernard DeVoto, quoted in a letter from Garrett Mattingly, November 23, 1956.

appointments he experienced in his home town. He worked from then on with a fantastic energy toward his new goal, symbolized somehow by his future home in Cambridge, Massachusetts, on Berkeley Street, just behind the Craigie House of Longfellow. His accomplishment lies in some twenty-five books and eight hundred short stories, articles, and book reviews. We think of him primarily as a historian of the early West with his works *The Year of Decision* (1943), *Across the Wide Missouri* (1947), *The Course of Empire* (1952), and his edition of *The Journals of Lewis and Clark* (1953). We think of him as a leading critic of Twain with his *Mark Twain's America* (1932), *Mark Twain at Work* (1942), and editions of Twain's writings in *Mark Twain in Eruption* (1940), *The Portable Mark Twain* (1946), and *Letters from the Earth* (1962). We think of him as the author of the Easy Chair essays in *Harper's Magazine* (1935-56), two hundred and forty-three of them, and the collected essays from many sources in *Forays and Rebuttals* (1936), *Minority Report* (1940), and *The Easy Chair* (1955). We remember that he was the editor of *The Saturday Review of Literature* for two years, that he lectured at Harvard and taught writing at the Bread Loaf Writers' Conference. We remember his attack on the F. B. I., his crusade against literary censorship in the *Strange Fruit* case, and his conservation fights. We have to add to this the several novels and the literary criticism in *The Literary Fallacy* (1944) and *The World of Fiction* (1950), and still we have ignored other aspects of his writing, such as the humor in *The Hour* (1951) and *Women and Children First* (1956). We are forced, of course, to the conclusion that he could never have done all this by staying in the West. He was transformed utterly in the years beyond 1922.

Did he late in life still think about the reaction of people in his home town? "I should certainly rather have them friendly toward me than otherwise," he wrote in 1945, "but

I have become so thoroughly a part of a different society that I am fundamentally indifferent." [7] There is no reason to question his statement, except, as Wallace Stegner has pointed out, "His repudiation of his western birthright would not stick; the West would not let him go so casually." [8] The historian Catherine Drinker Bowen supports the statement:

I could see why it was that a man of intellect and imagination had to leave Ogden, had to climb onto the Overland Limited, head east, and shake the dust of Utah from his shoes. Yet I saw also how, for the rest of his life, no matter where that Ogden boy might travel, to the Ultima Thule or the seven radiant cities of Antilia, he could not forget those startling deep canyons, that mountain air, and the glowing peaks where walked the gods of the Utes. Born and raised among those dry hard mountains a man must live haunted, his life dedicated to recounting the story of that country and of the caravans which traveled to it from the East. [9]

In the West were, as DeVoto acknowledged, "the sources of my thinking," [10] and the West was like an albatross around his Eastern neck.

There were first in the move from West to East some old scores to pay off. They partake of the phenomena of the Twenties which has been labeled the Revolt from the Village, and it was an attitude common to writers who came up from any Main Street of provincial America into the heady atmosphere of that other small town, Greenwich Village. Sherwood Anderson, Sinclair Lewis, Carl Van Vechten, Ezra Pound, Glenway Wescott, and even Willa Cather were engrossed with the crudities of their origins in order to clarify their new-found superiority. It was an American phenomenon, not a Western one, and DeVoto saw later but clearly the degree of his own involvement: "[I was] an over-sensitive young fool — and I had, or thought I had, been widely snooted and derided in

[7] Bernard DeVoto, "A Revaluation," *Rocky Mountain Review*, X (Autumn, 1945), 10.

[8] *Four Portraits*, p. 88.

[9] *Ibid.*, pp. 22–23.

[10] Bernard DeVoto, "Letter from Santa Fe," *Harper's Magazine*, CLXXXI (August, 1940), 333.

Utah for presuming to desire a career as a writer. . . . I re-
sented it violently. . . . So I reacted against it when I came
to write those articles. In some degree they were acts of self-
vindication, in some degree acts of revenge." [11] There were
only two such articles, one on Ogden and one on the Mormons, but such sentences as "How am I to suggest the utter
mediocrity of life in the New Utah?" and "No artist ever
lived there ten minutes after he had the railroad fare out" [12]
indicate the specific influence of the editor of *The American
Mercury*.

H. L. Mencken had taken the Northwestern University
teacher in hand — encouraging him, editing his work and publishing it, and transforming him. DeVoto explained the relationship: "As a critic and a friend he did so much for me that
there has never been a time when I should not have dropped
anything I might be doing in order to do anything he might
ask me to, and there was never a time when I did not furi-
ously resent his distorting my stuff with the clichés of his
own style and point of view." [13] The styles and attitudes of
the two men are not interchangeable, and a case might be
made on the basis of DeVoto's Harvard manuscripts concerning the prior influence of the *Yellow Book*, but the point to
make here is that DeVoto's "revolt" is Eastern in mood and
tone.

The move east involved yet another metamorphosis. While
DeVoto taught at Northwestern he published not only the articles in the *Mercury*, but also numerous book reviews and
two novels. Then he discovered *The Saturday Evening Post*,
discovered that he could write a story in three weeks' time
and sell it for $600, roughly a third of his teaching salary —
and he resigned from Northwestern in 1927. He was to pub-

[11] DeVoto, "A Revaluation," p. 8.

[12] Bernard DeVoto, "Utah," *American Mercury*, VII (March, 1926),
321. The other malicious article is "Ogden: The Underwriting of Sal-
vation," in *The Taming of the Frontier*, Duncan Aikman, ed. (New
York: Minton, Balch, 1925).

[13] Bernard DeVoto, "The Maturity of American Literature," *The
Saturday Review of Literature*, XXVII (August 5, 1944), 18.

lish about fifty stories and six serials, primarily in the next
eight years, and writing for the slicks became a major shaping force on his serious work, fiction or nonfiction. It was the
equivalent easy money of Twain's lecture circuit, and it made
possible the move from one social and economic class to
another.

DeVoto's stories in the *Post, Redbook,* and *Collier's* were
invariably constructed on the boy-meets-girl formula. They
made use of three environments which DeVoto knew well:
Harvard, Northwestern (called "Morrison" or "Olympus"),
and Ogden or Salt Lake City (called "Windsor" or "Custis").
The Western stories are built from the character of a cub
newspaper reporter and of a pioneer woman turned leader of
Windsor society; unfortunately they are nearly interchangeable with the stories of Northwestern or Harvard; if there
ever were any distinctively Western differences they have
been smoothed away. However, a character in a short story
of 1928 indicates well enough DeVoto's intent: "Here was a
candor, a realism, a satirical and sophisticated vision of the
West that could only have been a native's — yet a native who
was tempered by another birthright from older, wearier civil-
izations." [14] But in the process of publication, in the slick-
ness of their presentation, any such quality in the short stories was lost. There is the neat point here of something which
could not have been done by a native resident of the West or
by an Easterner either. We are reminded of that early
Twain title, "The Dandy and the Squatter."

DeVoto's novels are, like the short stories, more the product
of the East than of the West. Admitting that they are honest
and competent books, Wallace Stegner finds them lifeless
and literary; "The romantic idealist of the youthful letters,
the literary young man from Copey's class, shows through
more clearly in the novels than in any of the other writings." [15]
The Crooked Mile (1924) and *The House of Sun-Goes-*

[14] Bernard DeVoto, "Ranch Wondering," *The Saturday Evening
Post,* CC (June 2, 1928), 25.
[15] *Four Portraits,* pp. 101–102.

Down (1928) were, in fact, products of a scheme for a trilogy that dates back before 1920. They tell the story of the Abbey family in three generations: James, the pioneer of 1865, the farmer and land speculator; his son Pemberton, who develops a copper mine and smelter; the grandson Gordon, who returns from Harvard and the war to fight his home town. All three are supermen of great strength, energy, and sexual attractiveness; all three are romantic extensions of Bernard, his father, and his maternal grandfather. In this context they remind me of *Francis Berrian*, and of course as literature the two novels are failures, but whether from adolescent posturing or from the malevolent influence of Harvard is hard to decide. The attempt, however, is significant: to come to terms with one's own heritage, to acknowledge the peculiar formative factors of the West, to reduce the paradoxes of the Western experience to terms of reality and illusion, to discover at this early age that "poets, professors, and Presidents" [16] were responsible for two myths of the West — the Pioneer and the Frontier — which were in reality very different indeed from the myths.

Still another novel is pertinent, *Mountain Time* (1947), which stemmed from a serial in *Collier's* in 1946. This has a theme serious enough for literature, but unfortunately it was structured on the boy-meets-girl requirements of the slicks. It is the story of two disillusioned New Yorkers, a doctor who cannot tolerate the uncertainty and error of his profession and a woman whose divorce leads her to deep psychic perplexity; both, in 1920, return to their home, Custis, in the West. In the healing simplicities of their home town they find enough certainty to live by. Turning the pages at random, one finds that the base of the novel is much the same as in previous novels: "Disbelief has got to be your faith and you've got to dissect away illusion like old scar tissue!" [17] "What

[16] Bernard DeVoto, *The Crooked Mile* (New York: Minton, Balch, 1924), p. 23.
[17] Bernard DeVoto, *Mountain Time* (Boston: Little, Brown, 1947), p. 221. Further quotations from this text are not footnoted.

will any of us do when illusion runs out?" "Cy would destroy fictions if in the process he destroyed himself." In short, it is a major theme in a minor idiom, but the attempt is again significant in its confrontation of East and West, illusion and reality.

These are, of course, fitting themes for history and especially for history of the West, and they are the base for the history trilogy on which DeVoto's reputation will finally rest. His Western histories are syntheses organized on certain themes — thus, subjective presentations, literary in the finest sense. They are informed, enlivened by DeVoto's own firsthand experiences — or should his experience be called secondhand to distinguish clearly between knowledge of the present and knowledge of the past? Or is the proper distinction one of Western emotional attachment and Eastern intellectual detachment?

DeVoto's histories are an extension of his fiction in that as he grew older his writing moved progressively back into the past, probing for the distinctive causative factors of the present, for one's inheritance. They are in a very small degree an escape from the present. In this sense it is instructive to compare DeVoto with the preceding figures in this book. His effort is not at all that of a Nicholas Biddle, trying to see the West in purely Eastern terms, but it is like that of Lewis and Clark themselves, trying to record honestly a significant experience. DeVoto is not like Irving writing an entertaining sketch of the West; the contrast in intellectual depth is immediately obvious, though they share a tendency to romanticize, to color, in the evocative effort. He is not like Flint creating self-satisfying fantasies, using historical fact as the springboard for his heroic antics. He is by comparison with Twain more realistic, albeit nostalgic — as if whatever lay in the past is per se better than the things of the present. This is the mood shared with Cather, the tendency to find in history a satisfaction not in the chaotic present.

The Year of Decision purports not to be a Western history

but to show the forces implied in the term Manifest Destiny.

They had done that [DeVoto concludes], the people of this book: they had brought in that empire and made that war inevitable. The soldiers who followed Kearny to Santa Fe and on to California, Doniphan's farm boys and the Mormons slogging along with Cooke under their canopy of dust and miracle, Brigham Young's dispossessed people, and Owl Russell, Edwin Bryant, Jessy Thornton, the Donners. The wagon trains pulling out from Independence in the mud and coming finally to the Willamette or the Sacramento. They had shifted the center of gravity of the nation forever.[18]

The lives of these people are dramatized and patterned through the concept of empire. The passage goes on to remark the numerous spectacles of Western history and concludes with this interesting comment:

No Westerner, however, would begin the history of his region with spectacle. For the history of the West is the history of such people as we have seen here living out their lives in the new country, and watching their children and grandchildren grow up with that country. It is not a spectacular but a laborious history. One who once thought of writing it would have written it in terms of alkali, sagebrush, wind and water. . . . It could not possibly be a spectacular story.

The second history, *Across the Wide Missouri*, goes back in time to a spectacular period, that of the mountain men, concentrating on the years 1832-38. It is an even more lyrical book. In writing of the feast after a buffalo hunt, DeVoto writes a kind of poetry:

The firelight flares and fades in the wind's rhythm on the faces of men in whose minds are the vistas and the annals of the entire West.

It is the time of fulfillment, the fullness of time, the moment lived for itself alone. The mountain men were a tough race, as many selective breeds of Americans have had to be; their courage, skill, and mastery of the conditions of their chosen life were absolute or

[18] Bernard DeVoto, *The Year of Decision: 1846* (Boston: Little, Brown, 1943), p. 480. Further quotations from this text are not footnoted.

they would not have been here. Nor would they have been here
if they had not responded to the loveliness of the country and
found in their way of life something precious beyond safety, gain,
comfort, and family life.[19]

The nostalgia for the past is obvious.

The third history, *The Course of Empire*, surveys the Western explorations from the first Spanish in North America to
the arrival of Lewis and Clark at the Pacific in November,
1805 — the gradual displacement, by discovery, of illusion by
truth. Thus Coronado: "But there was no gold, no silver, no
emeralds, no lords of the country lolling in gondolas and
soothed asleep by golden bells, no golden plates and ewers.
Quivira was not a new Peru but only Kansas." [20] And the conclusion to the book:

From China and India but also from Cathay: on the far shore
were not only the Canton merchants who bought the sea otter but
Prester John and the Grand Khan who ruled kingdoms of marvel.
There had been but there would be no longer; for if this camp was
a beginning it was also a final end. They had filled out the map
and when the map is made there is no room or use for dreams. The
darkness into which the sentries peered till dawn was only night,
not the mystery through which for three centuries the mind of
western man had groped toward the horizon lands, the islands of
the sea, the Golden Chersonese, Anian, Quivira. Yet if the dream
faded from men's minds forever, this sleeping company who
had made a trail across America had fulfilled it. It had had much
beauty: they had brought it to completion. If they were the first-
comers to this shore they were also the lastcomers, and they had
been led here by all who had sought the fact in the dream.

Stegner, who knew DeVoto best and yet judges him so per-
ceptively, calls it "a three-volume history of the West as imagination and reality and realization." [21] The intuitive understanding in DeVoto came from his own Western boyhood;
the intellectual grasp of his subject is, of course, the product

[19] Bernard DeVoto, *Across the Wide Missouri* (Boston: Houghton
Mifflin, 1947), pp. 43–44.

[20] Bernard DeVoto, *The Course of Empire* (Boston: Houghton Mifflin, 1952), p. 45. Further quotations from this text are not footnoted.

[21] *Four Portraits*, pp. 106–107.

of his years in the East — and there is a kind of a tension between the two which is the source of literature.

History was one thing; lest I seem to accuse DeVoto of a retreat to the past, it is pertinent to cite his conservation activities as evidence of his unbreakable ties to the West. In the summer of 1946 DeVoto went west as part of his work on *The Course of Empire.* In the same summer, furious cloudbursts fell on the denuded watershed of Pleasant Creek, Utah, and cascaded a torrent of mud and rock into the town of Mount Pleasant. And in the same summer a Joint Committee on Public Lands with members from the American National Livestock Association and the National Woolgrowers Association met in Salt Lake City to consider ways and means of lifting the restrictions made by the United States Forest Service on national grazing lands. Overgrazing, of course, produces denudation and contributes to erosion-making forces; overgrazing is also a source of quick profit for the grazer. So the Joint Committee, with the help of a Republican Congress, would transfer national grazing lands to state administrations as the first step to private control. DeVoto was outraged at his discoveries of that summer, and his article "The West Against Itself" stopped the "land-grab" cold.

Some forty articles followed. DeVoto lectured the United States on various aspects of conservation in the West, and his articles were supplemented by lobbyist activities of an extent not yet publicized. DeVoto was literally one man fighting the cattlemen (Two-Gun Desmonds, he called them) who would overgraze and thus erode the national lands. A literary device is evident here; factors of erosion are much more complicated than the one-cause one-effect on which De-Voto harped in his articles. But with this device DeVoto was able to marshal diverse conservationists — and incidentally to further the split between the East and the West. This can be indicated with an amusing statement by the late Representative Frank A. Barrett of Wyoming (Republican), who spoke thus at a public hearing on the Forest Service grazing policies:

"So that just doesn't make sense, to be saying that cattle and sheep on the Wind River range are kicking up all this dust and causing all that silt down there on the Wind River, or up on the Missouri River in Montana. So it might sound all right in *Harper's* or in *Collier's* or some of these other eastern magazines but out here in the West it doesn't make sense to the people. . . . Why blame it on the poor sheep herder and the little old cowboy that's trying to make a living here on these hills." [22] DeVoto must have read this and roared at such evidence of his own bifurcation and dedication.

The literary point of this activity is an unfinished (and not to be published) manuscript *Western Paradox* on which DeVoto was working at the time of his death. There are first drafts of eight chapters which can roughly be described as follows: the illusions, contradictions, contrasts, and violences which define the Western paradox; the peculiar geography and climate of the West; the people of the West; the influence of the hardships and brutalities of frontier life; the mirage of the Old West; the Cattle Kingdom; and conservation. It was to be, in short, a cultural history of broad dimensions, absolutely unique in our literature of the West. The chapter on the mirage of the Old West, which was tentatively titled "The Eighth City of Cibola," appeared in print (in part and in different form) in an Easy Chair article on Owen Wister. Let us examine more closely DeVoto's point of view.

His thesis is that the cowboy story can never become serious fiction because of the myth of the Old West which Owen Wister invented. Wister went to Wyoming in 1885 and though he had the laudable ambition of chronicling accurately the social history of that time and place, he was unable to do so. He frequented the ranches of gentlemen and the Cheyenne Club and idolized Theodore Roosevelt. When he tried to publish a story in *Harper's Magazine* in 1894, describing a gentleman

[22] U.S. Congress, House, Subcommittee on Public Lands of the Committee on Public Lands, *Hearings*, Rawlins, Wyoming, September 2, 1947, 80th Cong., 1st Sess., on H. Res. 93 (Washington, D.C.: Government Printing Office, 1948), pp. 107–108.

rancher who in a fit of rage gouged out the eye of a horse, the editor of *Harper's* omitted the telling detail, and Roosevelt privately rebuked him for making literature disgusting. Thus Wister's *The Virginian* (1902) ignored reality and created a horse opera hero, "a sun god in leather pants"[23] whom subsequent writers have only imitated.

DeVoto made much the same point in an earlier essay on Westerns in general:

The novelist can have the Old West myth or the historical West but I judge that he can't have both of them at the same time. The actual prototype of the gun for hire was a repulsive psychopath like anyone who carried a submachine gun for Al Capone. . . . The odd effort of the novelist is not merely to make so much blood and gunfire momentarily acceptable as fast action, which the less ambitious Western does. It is to persuade us that we have witnessed some high human drama of aspiration and regeneration and atonement, and that the most admirable of human motives went into it, plus enough pure love to heal the wounds. It can't be done. Horse opera is kidding itself, and while it continues to nobody will take it seriously.[24]

Still another variation of the paradox emphasized the violence of the Western pulp stories and its source:

Usually there is an element of violence, which may be not overt but latent or perhaps only conceptual, and usually there is an element of fantasy, which may be apparent at first glance but is just as likely to be hidden deep down at the roots. The Western story tends to depersonalize man, and why not? — drought, blizzards, scalping do, the vast and empty Western landscape does. . . . Feeling his personality shrunk to miniature size by the enormousness in which it must exist . . . the Westerner has shaped his literature to a therapeutic purpose. In outline it is confession by avoidance, and usually it is self-derisive. If any of it appears to be simple, do not be deceived. The consciousness it expresses is complex, the basic pattern is intricate, the symbols are convoluted. The violence cannot be separated out from the fantasy, nor either of them from the inner derision. No doubt it is an admission of

[23] Bernard DeVoto, "Birth of an Art," The Easy Chair #242, *Harper's Magazine*, CCXI (December, 1955), 8.
[24] Bernard DeVoto, "Phaëthon on Gunsmoke Trail," The Easy Chair #230, *Harper's Magazine*, CCIX (December, 1954), 16.

defeat but what literature is not? And the self-scorn with which
the admission is made is at the opposite pole from self-pity. A man
who is laughing at himself is secure against the cruder indecencies
of fate, and if he is not a tragic figure, he has dignity.[25]

The final point of the joke lies in the Westerner's knowledge
that the literature is fake and romanticized. The trapper, the
Forty-Niner, the prospector, the cowboy "stand for innumerable magnificences which the West knows all too sardon-
ically never existed." But if the dude, the Easterner, wants to
romanticize the West, then this "sanctions the Westerner to
act out his dramatic fantasy artfully, not only derisively, but
with the heady knowledge that he is getting away with it."

Such are the paradoxes of the West which would have been
in DeVoto's new book. They are the paradoxes which made
up DeVoto himself as well. But the book was not to be finished. DeVoto went to New York to appear on a television
show, speaking of nature's power as a threat to modern civilization, and after the show he suffered a fatal heart attack.
The next spring, his ashes were scattered over the Clearwater
National Forest in Idaho, on the route taken by Lewis and
Clark.

The symbolic act brings us by retrospection back where we
began.

[25] Bernard DeVoto, "Two Points of a Joke," The Easy Chair #192,
Harper's Magazine, CCIII (October, 1951), 75–76. Further quotations
from this text are not footnoted.

8

FROM WEST TO EAST

It is typically ironic that the most recent study of the West should originate at Claremont College, California, and be published by the Princeton University Press: *Frontier: American Literature and the American West*, by Edwin Fussell. Professor Fussell argues that the concept of the West as developed in the first half of the nineteenth century is the key to an understanding of our early American literature and he presents in support meticulous studies of the West as metaphor in the works of Cooper, Hawthorne, Poe, Thoreau, Melville, and Whitman. The direction of his study is East to West, the opposite of mine, and it leads him to a casual, informative, but rather ridiculous statement: "No writer who lived in the West found much to say about it; and indeed, except as it came to exist in men's minds and imaginations, there was little to say." [1] I will have to disagree and say that the writer who lived in the West had a good deal to say about it and that there was in fact much to be said about the literal West, though of course I will agree that the concept of the

[1] Edwin Fussell, *Frontier: American Literature and the American West* (Princeton, New Jersey: Princeton University Press, 1965), p. 231.

West is important to the above-named writers. But I brood
about Fussell's next sentence: "Granted that Thoreau, and
the other major figures of the mid-century, lacked firsthand
knowledge of the West; at least they had the advantage of a
long perspective, and that advantage they capitalized on for
all it was worth and sometimes more." [2] *This* study concerns
firsthand knowledge, its necessity, and the failure of Western
writers to turn it to literary use.

The above-named Eastern writers certainly did not have a
firsthand knowledge of the West. The first three barely left
the eastern seaboard. Of the others, Thoreau had been to Minnesota in 1861, just before his death. Melville had been in
1840 at the age of twenty-one to the Galena lead mines in
northern Illinois, on the Mississippi (and from that short acquaintance with the river had written *The Confidence Man*).
Whitman had been, it is supposed, only as far west as New
Orleans. All that the six wrote, then, is based on the writings
of others or on their own imaginations.

Fussell did not study in detail the other major writer of
the period, Emerson, though his book is larded with references to him. (Fussell cites Emerson's comment, "At the Mississippi your Western romance fades into a reality of some
grimness." [3]) But of course Emerson was not of the West either. Two qualifications are necessary, for Emerson had been as
far as St. Louis as early as 1850 and he went to San Francisco
in 1871. On the first trip (and on a repeat visit in 1852), he
kept a "Journal at the West," a small pocket notebook recording statistics, impressions, even the sound of the voices
of people: [4]

"How did you get on with your goods. O you know the Pawnees
pitched into me & I was glad to get off with my scalp."

St Louis   Here they already smell the Pacific. A certain largeness
in the designs and enterprize of the people, generosity. They had

[2] *Ibid.*

[3] *Ibid.*, p. 184.

[4] Ralph Waldo Emerson, *Journal at the West, 1850*, MS 109a,
Houghton Library, Cambridge, Massachusetts, no pagination.

a boat drawing so little water that they said it would sail in a heavy dew.

St Louis   Mr. & Mrs. Dean at St Louis, told me, that they never knew what it was to live in a free country, until they came here. Here they are free.

It is fascinating to see Emerson so receptive to new experience, but as far as I can find, he made little use of this early material in his later writings. When Emerson actually crossed the West in 1871, he was too old for there to be any import on his writing. What we know of the trip is, in fact, the second-hand reporting of him by a member of the touring party. There are lovely anecdotes of Emerson meeting Brigham Young or riding a pied mustang or visiting an opium den, but only hints of the agile mind still hard at work. Crossing the edge of the Great Salt Lake, Emerson is reported as saying, "Well, what are you going to *do* about this, — all this beauty?"[5] But Emerson's main body of writing is not based on a firsthand experience of the West any more than that of the six other famous writers of the period.

The best writing of the first half of the nineteenth century was, of course, done in the East, and there is an obvious reason for this — if statistics have anything to do with it. The East in 1850 had a population of 23 million; the West in 1850 (using the seventeen states west of the tier of states extending from Minnesota to Louisiana) had a population of less than half a million, and would not reach the 23 million mark until about 1925. Unfortunately one cannot calculate the incidence of writers as a proportion of a total population, but this much is indicated: there weren't very many writers living in the West until some vague time after the 1890 closing of the frontier. It would take just one good writer to upset the statistics, but the point is that through the nineteenth century writing about the West was done by Easterners who had no firsthand experience or by tourists from the East. The

[5] Quoted by James Bradley Thayer, *A Western Journey with Mr. Emerson* (Boston: Little, Brown, 1884), p. 39.

West itself did not produce a great writer or even a good writer in its first hundred years.

In the twentieth century the West has produced (either with natives or emigrants) a wide range of writers extending from Willa Cather to Ezra Pound; but if the postulate holds good, if it is true that after 1890 the distinctive separate quality of the West was gone — Fussell gives a cutoff in the 1850's and 1860's, such that when Mark Twain arrived on the scene "the frontier and the West were gone" [6] — then the Western writers who would delineate their own country had no choice but to be retrospective and nostalgic, and per se second-rate. I am not ready to make axioms on such a flimsy base as this book, but my gloom deepens when I consider two recent fictional studies of the West.

Thomas Berger's *Little Big Man* (1964) purports to be the memoirs of a 111-year-old recalling his adventures in the West in the years 1852–76. It is, of course, a satire on Westerns, told with high humor, but it is derivative and lifeless. I am not sure the book was intended to be lifelike, though Chapters 2–8, dealing with the hero's childhood in a Cheyenne Indian village, are realistic enough. They are realistic because they are based on the incidents and descriptions of Parkman's *The Oregon Trail. Little Big Man* is a product of what Berger has read, not of what he has seen and experienced. No one pretends it is literature.

The other work of fiction is Clancy Sigal's *Going Away* (1961). Subtitled "A Report, a Memoir," it describes the cross-country trip of the narrator in 1956 from Hollywood to New York, his report on the bewildering America he saw, and his memories of his experiences in the 1930's and 1940's. Believing desperately in the destiny of America, yet finding in the complacency of the 1950's no continuity with the past, he sails for Europe. The direction, West to East, is of interest here, as well as the retrospective view — not just of the West but of all America. However, the book's opening scenes in the

[6] Fussell, p. 24.

Hollywood motion picture and television agency are a sufficient comment on the West and what there is left to write about. The West is no longer a foreign country; it contains no longer the promise of freedom for every man; and it has no significant literature of its own.

To go back, for a moment, to the original West and the possibilities inherent in it for a literature of its own. The matter is tied up with that other issue of nationalism or Americanism in literature. Since Jefferson and the eighteenth century our writers had been concerned by the shadow of England on our culture and called for an intellectual declaration of independence.[7] This is the note of Emerson's "The American Scholar" (1837) and later of a group of democrat writers of the 1840's, the Young Americans.[8] Such a charge was made in 1845 by the novelist William Gilmore Simms, writing on "Americanism in Literature": "[American writers] are European. The writers think after European models, draw their stimulus and provocation from European books, fashion themselves to European tastes, and look chiefly to the awards of European criticism. This is to denationalize the American mind. This is to enslave the national heart — to place ourselves at the mercy of the foreigner, and to yield all that is individual, in our character and hope, to the paralyzing influence of his will, and frequently hostile purposes."[9] Simms goes on with smoke and fire for several pages and then urges the American writer to a rather vague program of assimilation of his native environment: "The heart must be moulded to an intense appreciation of our woods and streams, our dense forests and deep

[7] See Benjamin T. Spencer, *The Quest for Nationality* (Syracuse, New York: Syracuse University Press, 1957).

[8] See John Stafford, *The Literary Criticism of "Young America": A Study in the Relationship of Politics and Literature, 1837–1850* (Berkeley: University of California Press, 1952).

[9] C. Hugh Holman, ed., *Views and Reviews in American Literature, History and Fiction, First Series, by William Gilmore Simms* (Cambridge, Massachusetts: Belknap Press, 1962), pp. 7–8. Further quotations from this text are not footnoted.

swamps, our vast immeasurable mountains, our voluminous
and tumbling waters." All this sounds rather like what I might
appear to be urging for a literature of the West. However,
consider the biting response of an anonymous reviewer of
Simms in *Blackwood's Magazine*:

But a national literature — will it come for any calling to it? Will
it come the sooner for the banishment of all other literature? If
Mr Sims [*sic*] makes his escape into the woods, and sits there
naked and ignorant as a savage, will inspiration visit him? Will
trying to *un*educate his mind, however successful he may be in
the attempt, — and he has really carried his efforts in this direction to a most heroic length — exactly enable him or any other, to
compete with this dreaded influence of foreign literature? [10]

America can no more *begin* a literature, no more start fresh from
its woods and its prairies, than we here in England could com-
mence a literature; neither can it any more abstract itself from the
influence of its own institutions, the temper of its people, its history, its natural scenery than we here in England can manumit
ourselves from the influence of the age in which we live.

Simms, the reviewer goes on, is free — free from "superior
genius, superior intelligence, from philosophy and taste . . .
free, and as barren, as the north wind." This too, that the
West cannot create a literature from nothing, is what I have
been trying to say here.

Almost immediately after this interchange (the British reviewer went on to praise Poe and Hawthorne), conditions
did change. America had its own distinctive literature — and
it was achieved not by separation from England but by an
intellectual development beyond England. Now, as we have
seen in the work of Flint and Hall, this same sort of Ameri-
icanism was called for simultaneously in the West — to separate itself from the East, from the domination of outmoded
ideas, manners, styles, loyalties, etc. — as if the West had a
distinctive life of its own. And there may be some validity in
this latter point, the validity of geography, the aridity and rock

[10] "The American Library," *Blackwood's Magazine*, LXII (November, 1947), 575. Further quotations from this text are not footnoted.

base of the West. It was easier to move England to New England than to move Emerson, say, to Nebraska (though there *is* a town named Emerson, Nebraska). The condition of life in the West, particularly in the nineteenth century, was a unique thing and there really was something to be learned by sitting there "naked and ignorant as a savage" — some harshness and breadth to existence not really present in the East — the sort of knowledge that so devastated Parkman. But, to the degree that this study indicates, the East refused the reality of the West, and the Western writers themselves concurred in the East's wish to treat romantically the concepts of freedom and individuality in the West. It is a consistent trend in the writers considered here, from Lewis and Clark to DeVoto, to accept the ideology, or at least the tastes, of the East. The firsthand experience was consistently altered to some lesser thing.

Still, this study has only begun to touch the literature of the West, and one must not presume that Western man was speechless. Simply to scan the literature leaves one with the impression that every single human being, man, woman, and child, has had something vital to say. This is not surprising from a country larger than Europe in a period of over a hundred and fifty years. And if a person didn't write a book, he sang a Folk Song or told a Tall Tale; if not that, he got shot by somebody in cold blood, and somebody else wrote the tale or sang the song. By now one ought to be able to carpet the entire West with books, and the only surprise is the consistent failure to reach a literary consummation the equal, say, of Emerson and Thoreau, Hawthorne and Melville. Perhaps there is something to what DeVoto says, that the scale of the West shows man his real size.

But I cannot end this study without at least mentioning some of the writers omitted, for with them another critic might well reach a different conclusion. Richard Henry Dana, Jr., in a good half of *Two Years Before the Mast* (1840), wrote about the West, wrote up the book from his journals and carefully edited down the strength of his language.[11] The other major case of downright censorship has already been mentioned — Owen Wister — but one should study the source which DeVoto only referred to, the letters and journal.[12] Such a work leads naturally to the fantasies of Theodore Roosevelt himself, in his *Ranch Life and the Hunting Trail* (1888) and *The Winning of the West* (1889–96). And one should compare his record of Dakota with that of O. E. Rölvaag in *Giants in the Earth* (1927) and *Peder Victorious* (1929), recalling the pioneer wagon with its woman tied into a chair lest in her terror of the land she might run away. Or compare the two records of Kansas, William Allen White's cheerful memoirs *In Our Town* (1906) and Edgar Watson Howe's depressing tome, *The Story of a Country Town* (1883). I cannot resist quoting the character Lytle Biggs: "Men who are prosperous, or men who live in elegant houses, do not come west, but it is the unfortunate, the poor, the indigent, the sick — the lower classes, in short — who came here to grow up with the country, having failed to grow up with the country where they came from." [13] One should, therefore, look at the Western record of that man who invented the catch phrase about going West, Horace Greeley, and that other reporter in the West, Bayard Taylor. Then one should survey the military or scientific records of men like John James Audubon, Lieutenant Zebulon Montgomery Pike, Major Stephen Long, John Charles Frémont, George Catlin, John Muir, John Wesley Powell, or Clarence King — and touch too that other area, the meet-

[11] See the Introduction to John Haskell Kemble, ed., *Two Years Before the Mast by Richard Henry Dana, Jr.* (Los Angeles: Ward Ritchie, 1964), pp. ix–xx. This unique edition has the 1838 manuscript version inserted by means of brown ink into the 1840 text.

[12] See the Epilogue to Fanny Kemble Wister, ed., *Owen Wister Out West; His Journals and Letters* (Chicago: University of Chicago Press, 1958), pp. 252–259.

[13] E. W. Howe, *The Story of a Country Town*, Brom Weber, ed. (New York: Holt, 1964), p. 210.

ing of King and Henry Adams in Estes Park (presented in *The Education of Henry Adams* like the meeting of gods in Valhalla). Having done that, one still would not have touched the diaries and journals, the memoirs of more ordinary people (Andy Adams, *The Log of a Cowboy*, 1903) or the distinctive tall tales of the Southwest.

In the twentieth century writers begat more writers. Even after we have set to one side a study which would take a lifetime — the cowboy literature, from the work of Eugene Manlove Rhodes through Zane Grey and down to Luke Short — we have left a marvelous variety. The West includes Katherine Anne Porter and John Steinbeck, Joseph Wood Krutch and Jack Kerouac, Robinson Jeffers and Phyllis McGinley. And it was to the West that Thomas Wolfe migrated just at the end of his life — what rhapsodies might have come out of that fatal trip? West, too, went Oliver LaFarge out of Boston to memorialize the culture of New Mexico. West from New York City went William Eastlake to make Indians talk like human beings for the first time in his *Go in Beauty* (1956). And then there is the work of a native of Texas which I would match with the best — John Graves, *Goodbye to a River* (1960), the narrative of a solitary trip down the Brazos River, a mournful, proud evocation of the past.

A chapter should be written, too, about Wallace Stegner, who was born in Iowa and went west to the prairie region of Saskatchewan, just north of Havre, Montana, and who wrote *Wolf Willow* (1962), "A History, a Story, and a Memory of the Last Plains Frontier." He handles as toys the problems of space and wind and sun. "I am not sure I would trade," he writes, "my childhood of freedom and the outdoors and the senses for a childhood of being led by the hand past all the Turners in the National Gallery." [14] *This* is the firsthand experience and the quality that for a time could only be found in the West — freedom and the outdoors and the senses — until it disappeared there too.

[14] Wallace Stegner, *Wolf Willow* (New York: Viking, 1962), p. 25.

The twentieth century did labor under the onus of the past, the fear that what was lost was somehow better than what remained, and a tradition of fantasy encouraged by the East's romantic notion of what the West *should* be. The poet Thomas Hornsby Ferrill blames the landscape and the writer's assumption that he must create superhuman males to match the magnitude of scale in the West — hence, loose ecstasy and low-grade mysticism, not concrete experience.[15] A recent study by Professor Wilson O. Clough of the University of Wyoming says all this better than I can. He asks why the West has produced no national classic. Rejecting the usual apologies of the youth of the country and the prerequisites of leisure and cultural stability, Clough emphasizes that a great literature emerges not from landscape but from the minds and emotions of a few gifted men and women. He looks on the appeals to landscape and the nostalgia for the frontier days as irrelevant and adolescent: "A sentimental nostalgia for this elemental past is of little use to those seeking esthetic maturity."[16] He finds, indeed, that the West has long been treated as an escape land, that it

utilizes as the symbol of freedom from conventional restraints, a happy irresponsibility, or, in its more austere solitudes, as surcease from anxiety, a stretching of the muscles, and a renewal of the will to live. This is humanly fine. But as such it is not enough for a great regional literature. It too nearly parallels the romantic age of nature worship, or the American tourist's delight in the baroque monuments of Europe at the price of a total ignorance of their cost in European history and politics. If the west were to be limited to this contribution alone, however pleasant in its way, we might well despair of a literature of power from its inhabitants.[17]

Clough would have the writer of the West steer between the Western stereotype and the Eastern model and consider, be-

[15] Thomas Hornsby Ferrill, "Writing in the Rockies," in *The Rocky Mountain Reader*, Ray B. West, ed. (New York: Dutton, 1945), pp. 395–403.

[16] Wilson O. Clough, *The Necessary Earth; Nature and Solitude in American Literature* (Austin: University of Texas Press, 1964), p. 156.

[17] *Ibid.*, pp. 157–158.

fore the concept of the free American becomes only a memory, the worth and dignity of man. It is time to mention — to emphasize the span between the greatest and the most recent — Kathleen Windsor's *Wanderers Eastward, Wanderers West* (1965). Time in the West may have run out.

Simms in 1842 made the point that history exists for literature. And Fussell points out that a writer by making a metaphor of the thing makes something more significant than the thing itself; Thoreau, for example, argues that the actual West has to be abjured in order to possess the essential West.[18] Fussell is saying that the symbol of the West is more important than the firsthand experience; I presume he would say that the *meaning* of Lewis and Clark is more important than that Lewis and Clark existed. Perhaps what my study means is that if the metaphor of the West had to be adjusted to the dimensions, the tastes, the modes of the East in its transformation from the basic document of experience to the ordering of literature, then the essential West was not in fact related to the actual West; and that the writers of the West, at least those studied here, lost in their passage to the East the very quality of innocence which animated them in the first place. And now, since the experience is past, I conclude that it has been lost for all time. There was this chance, you see (I combine and paraphrase the three writers on the reverse of the contents page), for the Western spirit to enlighten the world by the reversal of the East to West movement; but if the literature, the metaphor, did not relate to actuality, then it was simply not important to the mind of the time.

[18] Fussell, p. 194.

Bibliographical Notes

There are thousands of books concerning the American West, far beyond the reading capacity of any one person. Such a restricted and selective bibliography as Mabel Major, Rebecca W. Smith, and T. M. Pearce, *Southwest Heritage*, Albuquerque: University of New Mexico Press, 1938, lists 600 titles. Ramon F. Adams, *The Rampaging Herd: A Bibliography of Books and Pamphlets on Men and Events in the Cattle Industry*, Norman: University of Oklahoma Press, 1959, has 2,600 entries. A formal bibliography to my study would outweigh the book itself and give the erroneous impression that I had mastered all the available materials. The footnotes will have to serve to indicate the materials actually used, and these notes will indicate the bibliographical problems in each chapter.

From East to West. For all the historical concern over the frontier, there is no detailed *literary* study of the West. A brief survey is Henry Nash Smith, "Western Chroniclers and Literary Pioneers" in Robert E. Spiller *et al.*, eds., *Literary History of the United States*, 3 vols., New York: Macmillan, 1948; see also the bibliography in III, 264–269. There are some specialized bibliographies in certain anthologies. See John and Laree Caughey, eds., *California Heritage*, Los Angeles: Ward Ritchie Press, 1962, or Benjamin Albert Botkin, ed., *A Treasury of Western Folklore*, New York: Crown Publishers, 1944. A chronological literary bibliography of the West is a prerequisite to further studies.

Lewis and Clark. The best bibliography is in Donald Jackson, *Letters of the Lewis and Clark Expedition with Related Documents, 1783–1854*, Urbana: University of Illinois Press, 1962. The only purely literary study is Elijah H. Criswell, *Lewis and Clark: Linguistic Pioneers*, Columbia: University of Missouri, 1940. The most recent pertinent work is Richard Dillon, *Meriwether Lewis: A Biography*, New York: Coward-McCann, 1965. Historians tend to ignore the literary qualities of the journals, but it is precisely here that the two disciplines might help each other. If one were to place side by side in chronological order the existent journals of Lewis, Clark, Ordway, Floyd, Gass, and Whitehouse and study the borrowings of one writer from the other, one might be able to separate fact from fiction, fixing the events of the expedition with great precision. Such an edition is now called for.

Flint and Hall. Flint's fiction and nonfiction is probably less significant than Flint as a historical personage. John Ervin Kirkpatrick, *Timothy Flint*, Cleveland: Arthur H. Clark, 1911, good as it is, is unsatisfactory as a biography for the reason noted therein, the dearth of family papers. Some industrious Ph.D. candidate might consider the problem of Flint as a writer and a frontier phenomenon. The recent critical study of Flint's work, James K. Folsom, *Timothy Flint*, New York: Twayne Publishers, 1965, is far from exhaustive; its bibliography is selective. The two critical studies of Hall are excellent: John T. Flanagan, *James Hall, Literary Pioneer of the Ohio Valley*, Minneapolis: University of Minnesota Press, 1941, and Randolph C. Randall, *James Hall, Spokesman of the New West*, Columbus: Ohio State University Press, 1964.

Irving and Parkman. One is continually amazed at the "holes" in the literary scholarship on major American writers. Try to find, for example, how Irving came to write *Bonneville*. In regard to Irving on the prairie, John Francis McDermott, Stanley T. Williams, and Barbara D. Simpson have done careful research in the studies cited; but has anyone searched for the papers of Latrobe and Pourtalès for still more detail on Irving? The standard biography of Irving is Stanley T. Williams, *Life of Washington Irving*, 2 vols., New York: Oxford University Press, 1935. The studies of Parkman by Mason Wade and Howard Doughty both contain bibliographies. In neither work is there enough detail to explain adequately the wellsprings of Parkman's writings. We know next to nothing of the process of writing *The Oregon Trail*, surely a subject significant enough for some future doctoral candidate.

Twain. A complete study of Twain is the work of a lifetime, but there are still "holes" in our scholarship — the Iowa years, the Mississippi years, etc. One mourns again the untimely death of Dixon Wecter, the most able biographer of Twain. For a bibliography of Twain's early writing see Edgar M. Branch, "A Chronological Bibliography of the writings of Samuel Clemens to June 8, 1867," *American Literature*, XVIII (May, 1946), 109–159. However, the discovery of more materials in Henry Nash Smith and Frederick Anderson, eds., *Mark Twain of the Enterprise*, Berkeley: University of California Press, 1957, makes Branch's list out of date. Paul Fatout, *Mark Twain in Virginia City*, Bloomington: Indiana University Press, 1964, has a bibliography of some sixty books and articles on that short period of Twain's life plus numerous note references to contemporary Western newspapers — and Fatout admits that the day-to-day account of Twain in Virginia City is "fragmentary." The period of Twain in San Francisco is even less well documented. Even so, secondary materials have grown to such a bulk that no one has tried to absorb it all. More groundwork digging on the one hand and a new critical assessment of Twain on the other are badly needed.

Cather. The best study is still E. K. Brown, *Willa Cather, a Critical Biography*, New York: A. A. Knopf, 1953. The peculiar will of Miss Cather, forbidding the direct reproduction of her letters, makes a complete biography impossible. The University of Nebraska Press has scheduled for publication in 1966 *The Kingdom of Art, Willa Cather's First Principles and Critical Statements, 1893–1896*, edited by Bernice Slote; *The World and the Parish, Willa Cather's Articles and Reviews, 1893–1903*, edited by William M. Curtin; *Music in Willa Cather's Fiction*, by Richard Giannone; and a comprehensive bibliography of Willa Cather's writings, compiled by John March.

DeVoto. Catherine Drinker Bowen *et al., Four Portraits and One Subject: Bernard DeVoto*, Boston: Houghton Mifflin, 1963, contains a ninety-page bibliography assembled by Julius P. Barclay from the Stanford University collection of DeVoto papers. Garrett Mattingly, *Bernard DeVoto, a Preliminary Appraisal*, Boston: Little, Brown, 1938, is an excellent and early study, but too early to be inclusive. The Stanford collection includes an amazing 40,000 letters to and from DeVoto, but their use for publication is currently restricted by Mrs. Avis DeVoto. No literary history of the United States can afford to ignore this collection.

From West to East. Henry Nash Smith, *Virgin Land*, Cambridge: Harvard University Press, 1950, and Edwin Fussell, *Frontier: American Literature and the American West*, Princeton: Princeton University Press, 1965, are basic texts on the American West as symbol. One can hope that Wallace Stegner will write the literary history of the West which he alone can do, completing the unfinished work of DeVoto. Meanwhile see Wallace Stegner, "Born a Square — the Westerner's Dilemma," *Atlantic*, CCXIII (January, 1964), 46–50. The most recent study of the West is Kent Ladd Steckmesser, *The Western Hero in History and Legend*, Norman: University of Oklahoma Press, 1965. Steckmesser examines Kit Carson, Billy the Kid, Wild Bill Hickok, and George Armstrong Custer, comparing the Western facts with the myth-making work of Eastern journalists.

Index

Villagrá, Gasper Pérez de, 5–6, 8

Virgil, 51

Voorhis, Eleanor Glascow and Mrs. Julia Clark, 19

Wade, Mason, 69, 74, 77–78

Ward, Artemus, 92

Warner, William, 22

Wecter, Dixon, 84n, 96

Wescott, Glenway, 142

West: boundaries, 2, 83; population, 3, 155; size, 3

White, William Allen, 160

Whitehouse, Joseph, 14, 15–16, 19, 36

Whitman, Walt, 37, 153, 154

Wiener, Mrs. Charles, 116

Willard, Alexander, 22

Windsor, Kathleen, 163

Wistar, Dr. Caspar, 12

Wister, Owen, 150–151, 160

Wolfe, Thomas, 139, 140, 161

Woolf, Virginia, 113

Wordsworth, William, 51

York (William Clark's slave), 37

Young, Brigham, 147, 155

Young, Edward, 51

Zúñiga. *See* Ávila y Zúñiga